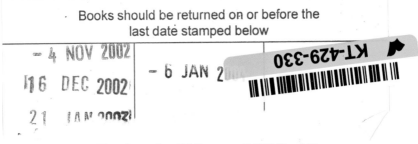
A Bairn's War - 1939-45

Jim Davidson

Published by Jim Davidson

"A Bairn's War - 1939-45" pubished by Jim Davidson 2002

© Jim Davidson 2002

Line drawings © Paul Davidson 2002

Printed by P. Scrogie, Peterhead, Scotland

ISBN : 0-9543108-0-2

CONTENTS

Chapter 1	Outbreak of War	1
Chapter 2	The first months of conflict	7
Chapter 3	The Gas Scare	13
Chapter 4	Spies - and our first bomb	19
Chapter 5	Flotsam from war	25
Chapter 6	"Careless Talk Costs Lives!"	31
Chapter 7	Backie Concerts and Bombs	39
Chapter 8	Invasion fears	45
Chapter 9	Casualties and Censorship	53
Chapter 10	First encounter with my future wife	59
Chapter 11	Bombing raids	67
Chapter 12	"A crime without a name..."	75
Chapter 13	Damage from friendly fire	81
Chapter 14	A bad beginning to 1942	89
Chapter 15	"Very Restricted Area"	97
Chapter 16	The fugitives	103
Chapter 17	The tide on the turn	109
Chapter 18	Twilight of childhood	115
Chapter 19	Good and Bad News	121
Chapter 20	Victory	127
Index of Civilian War Casualties		135

ACKNOWLEDGEMENTS

I am indebted to the staff of the Public Libraries of Peterhead, Fraserburgh and Aberdeen for their assistance in unearthing information of a bygone time which helped put memories into an authentic framework. And thanks to the many members of the public, too many to name, who told me of their wartime memories. A special thanks to Scrogie's Printers, Peterhead, for their practical and generous support, and to *The Buchan Observer* for recording so much of what went on in those long ago wartime days. Lieutenant Colonel I. Shepherd, Secretary of the Scottish National War Memorial Trust, Edinburgh Castle gave encouragement and practical help, and I thank him and hope he will look kindly on chapter 16. Derek Tucker, Editor of the *Press & Journal* gave permission to use their photographs on pages 35, 40, 51 and 71. Mrs Isobel Strachan of Glendaveny gave me a picture of her brother Jimmy and myself which I have used both on the cover and within the book. My son, Paul Davidson, did the line drawings and spent much time in researching to get the details accurate - I thank him. And finally, I thank my wife, Jean, who not only forgave the circumstances of our first encounter, but also supported me wholeheartedly in the writing and production of this book.

EXPLANATION

One Sunday morning in November a few years ago, I was at a Memorial Day parade. I looked up at the plinth and thought of all the real people represented by those names carved in the granite. Then it occurred to me that we had nothing to commemorate the civilians, the men, women and children, especially the children, who had died from enemy action in those war years – 1939-45. And some time later I learned their names were recorded in the Scottish National War Memorial in Edinburgh Castle. I checked that record, and from that early research grew the conviction that I had to write this book. So I wrote it.

Many who remember those war-time days have contributed to its contents, but I take full responsibility for any factual errors which may be found in it.

Jim Davidson

ILLUSTRATIONS

Concrete Shelter at Craigewan   32

Longate bomb damage   35

Academy bomb damage   40

Anderson shelter   51

A wee girl   61

"our Fire-engine..."   69

First Aid Post   71

"I was tall for my age..."   77

James Street, Peterhead   79

Ship in south harbour   85

"men of the lifeboat service"   91

Chapter 1

"Outbreak of War"

The summer of 1938 was brilliant. We had just returned to Peterhead after two years in Glasgow where my father and older brother, Willum, had worked in Fairfield's shipyard. We lived there in a place called Partick, and I started school at Dowanhill Primary School. Father and Willum had been building big boats. They'd worked on liners for Cunard and on two Navy destroyers, the *Maori* and the *Gurkha*. The *HMS Gurkha* had a busy but short time in the war and was the first British destroyer sunk by air-attack. This happened in April, 1940 during the Norwegian campaign. A bomb blew a large hole in its starboard side, and its guns kept firing until it sank. The *HMS Maori* was bombed and sank in Dockyard Creek in Malta in 1941, but nearly all the crew were ashore, so there were few casualties. I think both ships were launched in 1938, when father and Willum were at Fairfields, and although they were warships, we weren't thinking about war: 1914-18 was still too recent for the grown-ups. In Peterhead, we stayed with my mother's half-sister, Auntie Cameron, in Gladstone Road, and the braes and the seashore along beside the Killin' Hoose (Peterhead's abattoir) was our favourite playground.

Sometimes the tide was right in, and small waves broke against the steps leading down to the shore. The chingle made a continuous rustling as the waves washed the beach. The sea was clear and blue with pure-white foam, and the continually shining sun cast a spell over that beautiful summer. Our homecoming to Peterhead was a magical experience for a six-year old. Sometimes we played outside Brown's shoppie at the top of Gladstone Road, and since there was little traffic in those days and that was usually horse-drawn carts, the roadway was a safe playground.

A favourite past-time was bursting bubbles of tar on the road. If you got a match-stick, and there were usually plenty lying around, you collected the tar like a miniature lollipop, winding the black ooze round and round until it formed a perfect ball which gradually solidified but never hardened. And of course, you got tar on your hands and feet, or even worse, on your clothes and jimmies if you wore them. There was only one way to clean the tar off your skin, and that was with a buttery paper. I had often seen my father doing it to get rid of the paint from his work at the harbour - rubbing his face with the paper which shifted the small specks of paint. It was better for the skin than the turps; we used that for getting tar off clothes. I can't remember what we used to get tar off our feet - buttery paper or turps. And speaking of feet, that reminds me.

There was a day when we had been playing knights on chargers, or us small boys on the backs of bigger boys, and we had to hang on with one hand to our 'steeds' while we jousted with opponents and tried to haul the other riders from their perches. I say knights on chargers, though I don't think I'd heard of knights at that time. There was no TV in those days, few comics, and I can't remember hearing a wireless in the house, so there was not much chance of hearing about King Arthur and the knights of the round table. The only story I remember from the reading book at school was about a fox which persuaded a crow to open its mouth to sing so that the cheese the crow was holding fell to the waiting fox.

Anyway, whether we were knights or cowboys, and we had all heard of cowboys and Indians, I was up on my older brother, Alex's back. He was four years older than I and he towered alongside me. Disaster struck! I was hauled off his back. I landed on the stony tarmac and the granite chips tore the nail off my small toe. It was sore, bleeding and I howled. Alex shushed me so mother wouldn't hear, and the bleeding was stanched and I sat miserable and wounded on the pavement while the others jousted, though they were a wee bit more subdued. But I soon forgot my wound and it didn't bleed much, though it must have impressed me because I can still remember very clearly the warmth of the sun and my sore toe and Alex trying to shush my greetin.

Doon the Braes was wonderful, though one day in that glorious summer, the rocks and the sea were the scene of a great loss. Uncle Davy in Glasgow worked for the Cleansing Department, what we in Peterhead called the "scaffies". He and his work-mates went round during the night collecting whatever people threw out, and on one occasion, he "collected" a toy yacht. It was little use to him or his bairns living in the middle of Govan, but he gave it to us since we were going back to Peterhead. It was huge in my scale of things, about ten inches long with a deep keel, coloured red with a single mast and white sails. And we launched it in the sea at the back of the steps at the Killin Hoose and it was supposed to sail about for our pleasure and enjoyment. Which it did. And come back to us when we wanted it. Which it didn't. What a sad affair that was. There was an offshore breeze, and the bonnie white sails filled with the wind and our brave yacht headed for the open sea. The last we saw was it heading for Craigewan and Rattray lighthouse. Or maybe Norway. For I never saw it again.

Then came a bleak afternoon in December. I felt miserable as I struggled home from school. The world seemed to be falling in on me, and to make matters worse, one of my six-year old classmates took it into his head to pick on me. Perhaps it was because I was especially greety that afternoon. I couldn't be bothered defending myself, and how I got home I don't know. I saw that tormenter in later years, when he was a grown man and married with family and grandchildren of his own, but he's been dead a while now, and I wonder if he remembered that afternoon, and if he felt in any way responsible for me ending up in hospital. Because he wasn't to blame in any way.

When I arrived home hot and tearful, mother sent for the doctor and I was diagnosed - Diptheria. I didn't know what Diptheria was, but it was a killer in those days, one of the main killers of children. I can dimly remember lying in bed, awaiting an ambulance, and seeing yellow sulphur candles burning on the mantelpiece. Their fumes were supposed to kill the germs. The smell just about killed us. The only medicine I can remember getting that first night in hospital was a large glass of castor oil disguised as an orange drink. Sometime during the evening or night - the place was dimly lit and I had no idea of time or even where I was apart from a nurse sitting by my bed which convinced me I was in hospital - the castor oil took disastrous but predictable effect. I was mortified. And that nurse became a true angel of mercy.

It's easy to understand why some patients idolise their nurses and I wonder where she is now. December 1938, the Peterhead Fever Hospital, along by Buchanhaven. Are you still out there somewhere, nurse? You'd be an aul wifey now, but that night you were a true angel in nurse's uniform. Come to think of it, I must have been ill to have a nurse sitting by my bed... Nurse looked after me, cleaned me and the bed, and comforted me and in the morning I felt like wanting to live again. Breakfast came about 6am, porridge and a slice of bread spread with salty margarine. And I had to force it down, which I did, and I never looked back. The Diptheria was as good as licked.

Christmas came, but I can't remember if Santa Claus came on Christmas Eve or on Hogmanay night. What I can remember was that I was the only one in the male ward so I was moved in beside the wifies, and at six years of age, it didn't bother me. They spoiled me and it was all part of my healing process. That Christmas, by the way, I encountered Maltesers for the first time. They came in a small dark brown bag. And Santa brought me a book which I never read because the print was smaller than my reading book at school, and a flat box with coloured clay marbles you could put in various designs.

Soon after Christmas, I was released from hospital, and there at home the garland was still up, with my presents hanging from it. Santa had been especially kind to me and had visited both the hospital and Gladstone Road, so I had scored at both addresses. All the presents he brought me in hospital were left in hospital in case they had germs on them. So I had my stocking up all over again, and Santa at home brought me even better presents than he had in hospital, including a clockwork train. 1939 had arrived, I had lots of presents, and best of all, I was sleeping in our own bed behind my brother, Alex.

Spring of 1939, we moved house to Ives Park. We had been offered a council house up Hope Street, but it was too far for my father to get home at dinner-time from the harbour, so we exchanged houses with a Reekie family and we moved into their house in Ives Park. Our new house had a bathroom, and a garden for growing things, and a drying green at the back we shared with the Hamilton family downstairs. Our neighbours were friendly folk. There were no such people as "neighbours from hell" in those days, not in our part of Ugie Park and Ives Park. And there were crowds of bairns. It was a happy place to have your childhood.

Beside us was a cul-de-sac we called "The Blinner". And "the Blinner" was our football field, our race track, it was where we played "catching salmon" and "hanny oot", and "kick the tinny" and the girls played "beddies". "Doon the Braes" we fished for poddlies with limpets for bait, or searched for bandies in the rock pools, or turned over rocks for crabs. We lit firies and roasted limpets and boiled buckies, and when the girls were playing shoppies, we caught seaweed from the waves with ropes and a piece of paling wire twisted into a hook at the end, and the seaweed or "tungles" became fish we sold to the girls for pieces of sea-worn glass. The glass was either toffee or money, depending on the transaction. And the sun shone and it was a wonderful place for a six year old just coming up for seven.

My mother used to roast dulse we collected from the sea, a long frond of brown sea-weed. She roasted it by running a red-hot poker from the fire along its length. It was a custom from her child-hood in Cairnbulg, and she seemed to like it, but I tasted it once and never again.

That was a lovely summer, the summer of 1939, and we bairns played blithely ignorant of the rumbles of impending war. I wasn't even put out when my brother, Willum, joined the TAs and came home in his uniform. That was all part of the adult world which had nothing to do with us. He was paid a "bounty" or "blood money" as he called it, but the significance of that description had no impact on me.

What did have an impact was when my parents bought a wireless, an Ecko, with Willum's bounty money. We had music in the house and listening to the news became a daily ritual for my father and mother. And the *Buchan Observer's* editor gave his opinion that war was going to happen because of four important facts:

(1) Germany wants Danzig and intends to take it by any means

(2) Italy has promised to support Germany

(3) Poland refused to give up Danzig and said that if Germany tried to take Danzig, it would mean war, and

(4) Britain and France had promised to support Poland in resisting Germany. Though why we should go to war over a place called Danzig, I doubt if anyone in Peterhead could explain, not even the editor of the *Buchanie*.

War clouds were looming for our parents, but not on our horizons. If anyone mentioned war, it simply added an exciting dimension to our games. And then one Sunday in September, everything changed. Mother was stirring a pot of custard and I was waiting to see if Alex or I would get to "cla the pottie" - scrape the custard from the emptied cooking pot before it was washed. If you didn't get to "cla the pottie", you got a wee saucer of custard, but scraping it from the inside of the pot was better. Anyway, mother was getting dinner ready, the wireless was on, and Father was listening intently to it. We daren't make a sound. Things seemed different, and there was tension in the atmosphere. Then mother and father were leaning out the window speaking to people in the street. And mother was greetin.

A mannie named Chamberlain had said on the wireless that a state of war now existed between Great Britain and Germany. It had a disastrous effect on my parents. Everyone was very serious. And "claain the pottie" was not important. Now we began to understand why gas masks had been distributed in Peterhead a week or two before, 13,000 of them. And from that Sunday, a new influence had entered our lives, though we bairns made a game of it. Marching, saluting, shooting our rifles of fish-box wood, and copying the men going about the town in uniforms. They looked like strangers in their new appearance.

Later that Sunday, a German U-boat - the U-30 - sunk a passenger liner, the *Athenia*, north west of Ireland in the Atlantic. Of the large complement on board, eleven hundred of them civilians, 118 were killed either by the torpedo explosion or later in the sinking. Among the people on the *Athenia*, was the third radio officer who was a Mr R Ramsay, son of the

Congregational church minister at New Deer, and there was a Mrs Buckersfield whose father used to own a shop in Ellon. That was in the *Buchanie* three days later. For us bairns, war was something new, an exciting development in our childhood. But for some bairns in the north-east, and even in Peterhead, the war was to be deadly serious, so serious it would take them away and they'd never see the end of it, far less the end of their childhood.

Chapter 2

The first months of conflict

War was marching and saluting and shooting our make-believe rifles and machine guns, and charging each other, though we slipped easily from being Jerries and British into cowboys and indians, and back again. There were lots of dramatic collapses, shot through the chest usually, but you were instantly better if one of your own side touched you. So that was War for us in the autumn of 1939! Then came the time we had to try on our gas-masks. These had been issued in square cardboard boxes hung from our necks on a string. We got them at the old soup kitchen on Windmill Street just behind where the Job Centre is now. In the pre-war days, I made one visit to that soup kitchen with another boy who lived in Tanfield Close. He took a flagon to collect the soup on the way home from school at dinner time, and it was lentil soup. He let me taste it and it was good. My child's logic concluded that the soup kitchen made lentil soup and nothing else, though I suppose it must have had other varieties on different days. But I seldom have lentil soup nowadays without remembering that soup kitchen, and those long-ago days of hard-up families and their flagons of soup.

We practised putting on our gas-masks in school. Arms folded, we sat with the gas-mask in its box at our feet, then the teacher called out: "Gas-masks on!" And as fast as we could, we fastened them on to our faces, fitting the broad rubber straps over the top and the back. We got a telling off if we were slow in putting them on and she came round and pulled at them and tried to put her finger between the strap and our head. If it was slack, that was more trouble. The tight strap and the rubbery smell and hearing myself breathing and hardly being able to see through the perspex eyepiece when it fogged up are fresh in my memory. As an adult I was advised the way to prevent fogging was to spit inside the eyepiece, but I didn't know that then, and, anyway, the teacher would have had a fit if she saw us spitting.

The Police put a notice in the newspaper: "Always carry your mask and Keep Windows darkened." Father made large rectangles of black tarry paper stretched between wooden frames to fit our kitchen and scullery windows. That was a chore I did not like, putting up the blackouts. They weren't heavy - quite light in fact - but they were awkward, and once in place they were secured with wooden wedges. As winter approached, and darkness fell earlier, the blackouts had to be up before father and sister Jess came home from work. And if Alex wasn't in, I had to help mother. Or even put them up myself. Not a favourite chore.

The bedrooms, the "lavvy" and the lobby or staircase windows had no blackouts. They simply had curtains and were not blackout proof. I hated no light on in the "lavvy" for it was frightening for a wee boy to use the toilet in the dark. Of course, our lighting was by gas and you could hardly light the mantel every time you wanted to go to the toilet, but you could have left the kitchen door open a wee bit to get the light from the kitchen because the "lavvy" door had frosted glass panes in it. But no, that was not allowed. Light could escape from the lobby window as well as the "lavvy" window, or any of the bedrooms, if the kitchen door was left open. Then you would hear the ARP Warden shouting: "Put out that light!"

There was one Warden who couldn't get his tongue round the word: "light" and it sounded like "Put out that wight!" We dreaded that shout and if: "Put out that wight!" sounded of an evening, we would go into a darkened bedroom and peer round the curtain to see if he was shouting up at our window or someone else's. I can't remember him ever targeting our house, but maybe that's wishful thinking.

The lights which did escape from blacked-out houses were seldom from the actual kitchens or sculleries lit by their gas mantles, or blazing coal or shunner fires, but from light escaping down lobbies into bedrooms whose windows had no blackouts. Perhaps I should explain that in that far-off days, in council houses, we didn't use the term "living-room". It was the kitchen, where the family sat around the fireplace and listened to the radio and had their meals and entertained visitors. The scullery was what we would call the kitchen nowadays, and it had a cement floor with a boiler in the corner with a wee fireplace and mothers used it for boiling the clothes in. It had a tiny cupboard with a small window to the outside with a wire gauze over it, and that was the cold cupboard in the days before refrigerators.

One of the worst things that could happen in the blackout was for a chimney to catch fire. Such a fire would definitely attract a Jerry bomber who would drop a bomb down your lum. Maybe that happened elsewhere, but it never happened in Peterhead, though there was a story about it happening in Aberdeen later in the war. The way to prevent your lum catching fire in the dark was to make sure it caught fire in daylight, especially if it was raining and there was no washing hanging out.

And how was that managed, you ask? Our resourceful mothers knew how. They pushed a burning paper up the lum and it burned any soot there was, and quicker than you could say: "Mr Schickelgruber" - the chimney was clean and there would be no fire to attract the Jerries on a dark night. By the way, "Schickelgruber" was Hitler's family name, though we bairns thought it was a swear-word, one we were permitted to say, so we said it! In fact, I have a dim memory of Mr Winston Churchill in one of his speeches on the radio referring to "Herr Schickelgruber." We loved it.

Early in the first weeks of the war, the evacuees arrived in Peterhead and surrounding district. They came mostly from Glasgow and towns in the central belt of Scotland, which were designated by the authorities as likely targets for Jerry bombers, while the north-east of Scotland was a "safe area" for when the war got serious. Of that first influx of evacuees, I can't remember meeting any of them, though they all came to the North School, the school I attended. What happened was that the school closed for a week, and when it reopened, there was morning school for Peterhead children, and an afternoon school for the evacuees who had their own teachers. This timetable worked week about, each of us taking a "shottie" at attending morning school, then the following week attending afternoon school. And seldom the twain did meet.

I can't remember this arrangement lasting long, perhaps because quite a number of the evacuees returned south, though at the beginning it was mostly mothers with young children who left. But early in October, just weeks after the war had started, most of the evacuees had returned home and the Glesga accent was little heard in Peterhead.

That first winter of the war, everywhere was blacked out after dark. Going out was like the blind leading the blind, and what few motorised vehicles there were had special slatted and downward pointing head-lights so just a faint light shone down in front of their wheels. Bikes had similar though smaller lights, and their mudguards were painted with luminous paint so you could see them in the dark. There were also tin badges painted with luminous paint you pinned to your jacket, and they were supposed to let people see you in the dark. I don't know if they worked but you could play with them under the blankets in bed at night, and they really did glow, giving your faces a ghostly hue.

The Peterhead Townswoman's Guild took it all in their stride and they announced in the *Buchanie* that in future, their meetings would be held on evenings when there was a full moon. Bairns seldom went out after dark unless it was a special treat like going to the pictures. Or snow had started to fall and you wanted to experience the pleasure of throwing snowballs, and of course, when there was snow, there was a lightness about everywhere. It didn't seem so dark then.

Before the war, we used to gather round the lamp post and share ghost stories and scare each other with what was on at the Saturday matinee about the Clutching Hand or Frankenstein's monster, but those delights were at an end now there was a war on. War meant no gathering round the lamp post, because the lamp post was not lit, and would remain dark until Peace came again. It was an early victim of yon Schickelgruber mannie, Adolf Hitler, and one that hit us bairns badly.

In October of 1939, we heard that Jerry bombers had attacked the Forth Bridge and been driven off by our ack-ack guns. "Ack ack" was a military way of saying anti-aircraft and we practised showing off our knowledge of military terms. That raid was of special interest in our family because brother Willum was in the Royal Artillery and he was stationed on an island in the Firth of Forth named Inch Colm. And there was supposed to be a ghost on the island, but that's another story.

Willum told us when he came on leave of one of the Peterhead soldiers with the Royal Artillery on the island who woke one morning to find a large piece of shrapnel lying beside his head on the pillow. It had fallen beside him during his sleep and burned a hole in the pillow. He had slept on, inches away from death.

Meanwhile at school, we were told that if the siren went, we would be sent home. You can imagine how we looked forward to the welcome sound of an air-raid warning, our passport to a free day, though we were supposed to go back to school after the All Clear. It seemed not everyone was sent home from school because my wife, Jean, told me many years later that as a wee girl her class sometimes remained in school and she would sing to the teachers in their staff-room during an air-raid.

About this time word went round that fishermen's wives were being asked to make camouflage nets. My father wasn't a fisherman, but mother had come of fishing stock, her home village being Cairnbulg. So mother volunteered to make these great big nets. What I didn't like about them was they were made of hairy twine that felt almost like wire. And the twine came in big balls which had to be wound on to their needles which were long and flat with an opening in the middle with a prong sticking along it. That isn't a very clear description, but they were difficult to describe. And Alex and I had to wind the twine in and out and around the needle with each turn over that sticky out bit. And it had to be tight or else it made it difficult for mother when she was "wiving the nets."

There wasn't much room to move in our kitchen when the net being "wived" hung from the scullery door right across the floor, then when it was finished, mother would check it for mistakes, but she was pretty good and I can't remember any disasters in her wiving. Usually on Saturday morning, Alex and I had to take the finished nets in a barrow to a net loft down by the South Harbour where it was checked and weighed and we would get more balls of twine for more nets. I have no idea how much mother was paid or how she was paid, but I can remember that great long net loft and the piles of nets being bagged for sending off. On our way home again we usually went in by the gasworks to see if we could get a bag of shunners for the fire.

The bags of shunners were huge and light and sometimes warm and smelling of gas, and they were cheap, and they made a lovely fire. Not much flames, but going red hot and heating the water boiler up so that it bubbled and you could hear it through the wall. I can't remember if the shunners were rationed, but I do remember going into the gas-office just inside the gate to pay for the shunners and getting a slip of paper with a number on it and you gave that to the man who stood beside a huge pile of shunners and he shovelled them into a large weighing pan that was tipped into the bags once it out-weighed the weights.

The outstanding thing about that gas office was the linoleum on the floor shining like glass and gleaming brass-work, and the whole place smelling of gas. It was a frightening place, and a child could easily imagine dark scientific secrets happening there. In later years, I saw it as an ordinary rather shabby office, though the lady who worked there was always friendly and cheerful, and not in the least bit sinister. The shunners, by the way, was what was left when the gas was extracted from the coal.

Later in the war we would see mother's nets or others like them, but now dyed green and brown, and hanging over big guns along the Braes beside Buchanhaven. I suppose those camouflage nets went to gun sites all over Britain and perhaps overseas, maybe even to North Africa, but to us, they just meant sore fingers from winding the coarse twine on to their "wiving" needles and pushing a barrowload of netting down to the "mannie in the fish laft" at the harbour.

Rationing was introduced and our mothers had to register with shops where they wanted to buy their bacon and ham, and butter and sugar. Our favourite shop was Reid's Shoppie at the top of the second street in Ugie Park, though on occasion we would walk another block to Pat's at the top of the third street. That was a whole lot further and as bairns we preferred having to go for the 'messages' to the nearer shop. And as for Buchanhaven, that was an affa distance to walk, but usually it was to Bob the Baker or to Muggie Hooja's for a newspaper, though we didn't mind that if it included the rare treat of a **Dandy** or **Beano**. And that reminds me of a question I've often wondered about: when the **Magic** comic was launched and mother bought a copy for Alex and me, how did the comic manage to give away a small lollipop with the introductory copy? I could have sworn sweeties were rationed from early in the war. In fact, I remember when war was first declared that I saved up about half a dozen assorted sweets to enable me to cope with the wartime shortages that would come. Though my cache of sweets only lasted a day or two.

But as far as the free **Magic** lollipop is concerned, I suppose an even bigger puzzle is how my brother and I managed to cope with one comic and one minute lollipop, or did mother buy two comics, and so get two lollipops? I wouldn't put it past her if she had. And what happened to the **Magic** comic, anyway? When did it cease publication? I really enjoyed that comic.

Chapter 3

The Gas Scare

So 1939 was drawing to a close. It was a dark, dreich winter, with unlit streets and already shortages in the shops. The favourite 'put-down' for anyone who asked for something in short supply was: "Don't you know there's a war on?" There was no answer to that, though our mothers never said it to us bairns - their main concern was sheltering us from the harsh realities of wartime life, and fathers were forever thinking of ways to keep us safe if and when the Jerries bombed us. There was no thought of an invasion, for it was taken for granted the Jerries would get beaten just like the last time, but he would be nasty and kill as many as possible before he got his just desserts.

The Town Council put up the price of the gas it made in the gasworks down in the Longate. And since coal-gas was the main source for cooking and lighting the houses, that meant a cut in ordinary people's budgets. That didn't make much difference for bairns though it probably meant less money for celebrating Hogmanay. Thank goodness Santa, or Sunty, as we called him, didn't need money.

When we lived at Auntie Cameron's in Gladstone Road, Alex and I had gone to The Salvation Army Sunday School, but the bairns about the Blinner went to an Open Brethren Sunday School in Prince Street, so we left the Army and went to the Brethren with our new pals. I think I preferred the Salvation Army because we occasionally got a 'magic lantern' show there. The 'magic lantern' was a kind of primitive slide projector, but it was a wonderful thing to see those coloured pictures coming up on the big white sheet and it was 'magic' for us.

On one occasion in the Brethren all the little boys and girls who wanted to die for Jesus were asked to stand up, and everyone around me stood but I remained seated despite a bit of pressure from my peers and the teachers. I refused because I had no desire to die and I had taken them literally that if we stood up, we died. Our attendance at the Brethren continued until we went to a party in the run-up to Christmas. As much as I can remember, it was a decorous affair, and then suddenly the air was filled with flying buns. I was dumbfounded and hid below a seat to dodge the missiles, then my brother Alex hauled me to my feet and dragged me out of the hall. Outside, the children from Ives Park and Ugie Park were running like mad and I was dragged along with them..

What was happening? I had been enjoying myself though I thought all that buns flying about was a bit of a waste. And when I wanted to go to Sunday School next weekend, my pleas were rejected. We could not go back to the Brethren Sunday School, ever again. And it was not until I was an adult that it occurred to me that the bun fight was not on the planned entertainment for the Christmas party, and suddenly the innocence of decades was drawn aside like a curtain and I realised why Alex ran hell-for-leather up Prince Street dragging me after him and I could never go back to the Brethren Sunday School. We had been part of a riot...

We occasionally went to the picters on a Saturday afternoon, though I didn't get to see Shirley Temple in "The Little Princess", which is what the **Playhouse** had on offer when it stayed open all day on New Year's Day, 1940. I can remember only a few films from the wartime and they were mostly about the war, though there was one I was tricked into seeing at the **Regal.** I was assured it wasn't scary as it was about someone's mother - "The Mummy's hand" it was called - and it was a shock to my tender years. I spent most of the film cowering down behind the seat in front.

The Buchanie told us about "The Sign of the Beast". No, that wasn't a reference from the Bible or its Book of Revelation. That was the character of the Germans. They were all marked with the Sign of the Beast. And what is more, they were all the enemies of God. There was a lot of propaganda flying about in those days, and I wonder now if our parents believed it. For example, it was in the papers that a scientific study had proved the "Blackout" was good for our eyes. I think the idea was that our eyes would be rested in the dark and be better able to handle daylight. That sounds nonsense to me now. Meanwhile *The Broons* in *The Sunday Post* were doing their own bit about the blackout and the War Effort. They had been forced to stay in because of it, and make their home entertainment, playing snakes and ladders and table-tennis and "Postman's Knock" with Joe and Hen's soldier pals. Needless to say, the "Postman's Knock" was Daphne's idea - and poor Maw and Paw had to leave their game of draughts and go out into the blackout to get peace and quiet. The last drawing on that particular page was just a black square, a real blackout picture, with two conversation bubbles which said: Paw: "Ye canna get peace in yer ain hame, the picters are a' full up - whaur are ye, Maw?" Maw: "I'm here, Paw! Haud ma hand!" That's how black the blackout was.

We thought it funny, because it's best not to take things seriously all the time. There was a war on, but in 1939, it was more an inconvenience than anything else. As 1939 drew to a close, our war on the Home Front was mainly about blackout and shortages and complaining about how bad the Jerries were. War for us meant so many fathers and brothers had gone off to fight, but our only experience of the Jerries was in our children's comics and *Oor Wullie* and *The Broons.* But that was soon to change, as 1939 gave way to 1940.

With the new year, began a very determined propaganda campaign for the hearts and minds of the public, and the goal was to make us all hate the Jerries. Someone wrote to *The Buchan Observer* describing himself as "A Citizen of the World", and he had the cheek to say that the German people deserved the sympathy of the British people because of the badness of the German "leadership of Hitler and his associates." Sympathy? The floodgates of anti-German feelings opened. "A Citizen of the World" had stirred up a hornets' nest, and resentment against him and the Germans came in a swarm encouraged by the newspaper's opinion column and readers' letters poured in condemning this "Citizen of the World." There was no doubt about it and dare anyone say otherwise: the Jerries had the leaders they deserved and - "the only good Jerry was a dead one". "A Citizen of the World" indeed. Huh!

Looking back with decades of hindsight and cynicism fuelled by knowing how propaganda works, I suspect that "Citizen of the World" was someone in the British Ministry of Information whipping up anti-German sentiment. And it worked. But we bairns didn't need propaganda in the press. Probably wouldn't have understood it any way. We had already lumped all the Jerries together with red indians and cowboys who wore black clothes and rode black horses and shot people in the back, and with Emperor Ming and the claymen in the Flash Gordon serials on a Saturday afternoon at the picters. They were all "bad eens", and of all the "bad eens the world ower", the Jerries were the worst.

Early in 1940, the Jerries were affecting our lives a bit more. Off Peterhead, we could see the convoys of big cargo boats with their barrage balloons floating above them, and the destroyers and corvettes and other boats escorting them. And whenever German bombers attacked them, if it was during daylight hours, we would watch them on the distant horizon. It was like it didn't affect us, but of course it did, because whenever a raid was on, the town's Air Raid sirens went. If we were at school, we were sent home, so for us, the first effects of a raid at sea was a welcome break from lessons. But if it happened after dark and we were in bed, we would be hauled awake and forced to dress and seek shelter, and that was not so good. And if we didn't get a good night's sleep, we'd be grumpy next day.

Though the horizon at sea was about twelve miles away, we could hear the thump of bombs dropping, and occasionally detect the distinctive sound of the German engines. British plane engines made a steady buzzing sound, while the Jerries made an undulating Vroom-Vroom-Vroom. That sound is forever linked in my mind with those German bombers. It was something to do with their type of engines.

There was a bit of buzz in the town because Peterhead was mentioned on the news. A tanker had been bombed and brought safely into the shelter of Peterhead Bay. So for us in Peterhead, we could see the war happening, but it was happening about twelve miles away, apart from that tanker in the Bay. Sirens became commonplace, but so far not a bomb had fallen on the town. And the Sirens had their distinctive sounds. The Warning Alert was a wailing sound which rose and fell, making the hair stand on the back of your neck. The All Clear was a friendly steady sound, no going up and down. And for a while, that was the only impact the Luftwaffe bombers had on us. We had learned to pronounce the word: "Luftwaffe", though we couldn't have spelled it.

RAF airfields were being built around Peterhead, mainly at Longside and Crimond. Peterhead men who couldn't go to the forces for one reason or another, perhaps for health reasons or were too old, or even too young, were getting work building the airfields. And there was an influx of Irish workers from the Free State as it was called, Eire. They were not involved in the war because they were neutral and they came to Peterhead and lived mostly in camps outside the town.

Spitfires began to appear more often in the skies over Peterhead though to our inexperienced eyes, every one-engined British plane was a Spitfire, and they could have been Hurricanes or Defiants and we wouldn't have known the difference. These planes were mainly to protect the convoys sailing past Peterhead, for convoys from America sometimes came round the top of Scotland on the way to East Coast ports.

After we were introduced to the Spitfires, all the loons became Spitfires, and we would chase each other with arms outstretched rat-tatting away, our imaginations at bursting point. But since no one would admit to being a Jerry, those dog-fights even in a crowd were very much isolated affairs.. everyone a "guid een" - a Spitire, and no one ever shot down. The Spitfires were always victorious. It was just like the newspapers said when they praised the superiority of the Spitfire over the German planes whose names we didn't know or if we knew of them, couldn't pronounce. At least, not that early in the war, although it wasn't long before we learned their names. I saved up my Saturday pocket-money to buy an airplane recognition book. Soon I was familiar with names such as Heinkel and Dornier and Messerschmitt and Stuka. And the British planes: the Spitfire, the Hurricane, the Bolton Paul Defiant, the Lysander and the Wellington bomber. Nowadays I see young people who can tell you all about their pop idols or football stars or Godzillas or Pokemons or whatever - for us wartime bairns, it was the names of planes and tanks and guns.

Then came the Mark of Zorro - Tyrone Power, the greatest swordsman in France. He was the craze for a time, and Zorro played havoc with the slatted wooden fencing round the council house gardens. If you fitted a slat through the lid of a Mansion Polish tin it made a brilliant sword, though you were supposed to turn the sharp rim of the lid away from your hand and toward your opponent. I learned that the hard way, because I had the sharp edge of the lid pointing toward my hand, and when the sword of an opponent thwacked down on it, instead of protecting my hand, the edge cut deeply into my wrist. I still have the shiny scar to remind me of the time the greatest swordsman in France got a bleedy hand. Looking at it as I write, I see it missed a vein by about half an inch. But it didn't deter us from our sword fights. I simply turned the polish tin lid to face the other way and fought on...ta raa!

People began to collect things for our boys at the front or on the convoys. Books and scarves and balaclavas and socks. Mothers were forever knitting. If it wasn't camouflage nets, it was woollen things. I caused my soldier brother some hilarity by knitting him a scarf, which had more than its share of dropped stitches. That was my only attempt at knitting, and it was a bit narrow and not too long. But as he said, it's the thought that counts.

Sometime early in 1940 we had a gas scare. We had our gas masks so we bairns thought it was just a matter of time before the Jerries tried to gas us, because they were the "bad eens". Gassing was a kind of "cheaty thing" to do, but that was what you could expect from Jerries. Then the *Buchanie* issued advice on what to do if you were splashed with Mustard Gas. We had all heard of Mustard Gas because the Jerries had used it against our soldiers in the Last War, in the trenches of Flanders or France or wherever. And men came back from it with bad lungs and worse coughs, if it hadn't actually killed them. So we had all heard of Mustard Gas though it was a puzzle to us trying to connect that yellow stingy stuff our parents put on their food with a German gas.

How to deal with Mustard Gas? Straight from the Government through our local newspaper came the advice: Splash raw Parazone bleach which contains chlorine on to the part of us which has been touched by the Mustard Gas and keep on doing it until all the Gas is off you, then wash well the affected part until all the Parazone is off. There was no advice about what to do if you swallowed or breathed in the gas. Probably you'd be dead. But would the Parazone treatment have worked? I wonder.

Anyway, it's no wonder with all the advice about gas and getting the gas-masks and having to practise at school putting them on, that we were fully expecting a gas attack at anytime. And so it came, as we thought.

We bairns from the Blinner had gone in a crowd along the railway line which ran down to the coal depot next to the slipway at the harbour, with its wee spur leading into the Killin Hoose. The Camerons' dog, Fido, was with us. He'd been dragged away from a fight with another dog to accompany us on our foray, though where we were going and why, I can not remember. It must have been something important, important to us that is, because we were at full strength and we had Fido.

Then one of us noticed our knees. We all wore short trousers with stockings up to our knees though they were usually down around our boots. Anyway, he was staring goggled eyed and pointing and we looked. And there it was. All the evidence of a gas attack. Our knees were speckled with blood. We were dying. Mustard Gas! We forgot our important journey, and ran for home, with Fido lolloping along beside us, enjoying the excitement. We had one thought in mind - home to our mothers and warn them about the gas. And get made better.

Until someone shouted: "Stop!" He was pointing at Fido. A piece of Fido's ear was hanging by a thread and he was shaking his head and every time did, he spattered us with blood. That was our "gas-attack". We had a laugh about it and Fido was taken home for medical treatment and as far as I know, that was the last "gas attack" on Peterhead or anywhere else in Britain.

Chapter 4

Spies - and our first bomb

Early in 1940 we heard about a Fraserburgh fishing boat, the FRS120 *Sisters* with a two-man crew. It had been on the fishing ground when it was strafed by a German bomber. There wasn't much the crew could do about evading the attacks, but it managed to dodge the Jerries and they never scored a hit on it. One bomb on target would have blown it to match-wood but it came through the attack unscathed, apart from a bullet hole in the wheel-house. The success of the Broch boat just went to prove we were better than the Jerries any day and there was no way we wouldn't win the war although judging by the newspapers and the news on the wireless, it wasn't much of a war anyway. They were calling it the Phoney War, meaning nobody was fighting. Apart from the crew of the FRS120. And theirs' was a morale-boosting victory for the folk of the north-east, though looking back from today's perspective, I wonder if the crew of the bomber were trying all that hard. Perhaps it was just a half-hearted target practice for the Luftwaffe.

About the same time, at the beginning of March - just in case we thought it really was a Phoney War - there was in the *Buchanie* the report of a Peterhead sailor being killed when his navy trawler was sunk by a German bomber. He was 24-year-old Alexander Watson of Dingwall Drive, and from now on, lists of casualties appeared every week in the *Buchanie*. It didn't make much of an impact on bairns though we could see our parents were worried, and in a small town like Peterhead where nearly everyone knew everyone else, or at least knew their family connections, those lists each Tuesday made a personal impact. Most families had someone away in the "sojers or the raff or the navy."

German bombers were killing people in other places. In Aberdeen, a John Stewart of North Anderson Drive was injured in Loch Street, and he died in hospital two days later. He was the first civilian in north-east Scotland to die from German bombing. The *Buchan Observer* never actually gave the names of towns or places which had been bombed. It always said: "a town in the north east" - and that included Aberdeen which was a bit big for a town, and even when it mentioned our home town, the **Buchan Observer** never said "Peterhead" but always "a town in the north east of Scotland." I could hardly believe the Jerries didn't know where they had been. But censorship has its own logic.

Posters appeared on walls and up in the railway station, posters announcing: "Careless Talk Costs Lives". Another one called on every-one to: "Dig for Victory". That meant every bit of spare earth should be dug over and something for food planted in it. My father had a bizarre idea in the spring of 1940, and I never heard of anyone else in a council house doing it, so maybe it was unique to him. He decided to grow oats in our garden, a tiny field of waving golden corn, about four yards wide and twelve yards long. It was a bonny sight in the late summer, and it was a tempting place to hide in for our games, but we seldom went into it because that would flatten it and make it useless. And even as bairns, we knew that would help the Jerries. Young and old, we shared the community spirit of doing everything possible to beat Hitler and not doing anything to help him. Everyone, even the youngest, wanted to beat Hitler.

That may be a lesson for us nowadays, when contemporary society seems to be fractured and pulling different ways. It may be that we need a community awareness of a common enemy, someone or something we can unite against. It worked in the war years, and it struck a chord in a fundamental part of human nature, so it might work again today.

Back to our "field of corn"...when harvest time came, my father could-n't do anything with it, but he made a deal with the greengrocer who came round on a Saturday with his horse and cart, and that gentleman cut it down and took it away in bags, and gave us a bag of potatoes in exchange. For the rest of the war, father grew potatoes in that garden, just like our neighbours, but in 1940, our potatoes came in a sack from "the vegetable mannie" not the garden. While the mannie's pigs probably dined high on our corn. Or maybe the mannie and his family did.

Spring of 1940, nothing much seemed to be happening at the war-front. They called it the "phoney war" and any fighting was in a place called Finland. I remember the **War Illustrated** every Saturday and it was full of pictures of soldiers dressed in white and the brave wee Finns were putting up a great fight against the big bullies, the Russians, though everyone thought the Finns would get beat in the long run. And so they did but they made the Russians pay a very heavy price in war-dead, almost ten Russian soldiers killed for every Finnish soldier. It was from magazines like the **War Illustrated** or the **Picture Post** or the **Weekly Illustrated** (I think that was its title but since it ceased publication early in the War I can't be sure, though it was the first of those style magazines to use full colour pictures) that we bairns learned the names of the different weapons and the vocabulary of War.

One piece of good news during this time of Phoney War was when one of our destroyers, the *Cossack*, captured a German ship crammed with British seamen prisoners from vessels sunk by the *Admiral Graf Spee*. The Jerry boat, the *Altmark*, was captured in a Norwegian fjord, and the Norwegian government wasn't happy with the Royal Navy because Norway was a neutral country. But if it was neutral, why did it allow the Germans to keep British sailors as prisoners. It's a funny world, too difficult for adults to understand, never mind bairns. But it didn't matter in the long run because Germany invaded Norway and the Norwegians came on our side anyway.

During the Phoney War, we had our occasional moments of excitement on the home front, though not as exciting as for a farm-worker at St Fergus who found a live shell and thought it was a part fallen off a motor car. He found it in the middle of a field of all places. It was obvious he hadn't been reading the *War Illustrated* or he would have recognised it as a shell. Any Peterhead bairn could have told him. Anyway, the other farm-workers knew what it was and chased him off to report it to the police. It must have been a shock for him to learn he had been carrying a live shell about with him under his jacket. But it shows how working-folk knew so little about motor cars that he mistook a shell for a piece of a car.

About this time the Local Defence Volunteers was set up. This was a home defence army of men and boys who did not qualify for the regular forces. They didn't have uniforms to start with, just arm bands. And they didn't have weapons. There was a rumour they did their arms-drills with sweeping-brush handles. I don't know if that was true, but bairns did not take them seriously. Very soon, the LDV which they were called, were known as the Look, Duck and Vanish brigade, though the newspapers called them the "Parashots". I suppose it was unfair to poke fun at them, but we bairns thought they were playing at soldiers since they had neither uniforms nor guns, though later on they did get Lee-Enfield rifles from the First World War.

If we had imagined there would be no need for the LDV, the events of the summer of 1940 proved otherwise. The Germans suddenly came alive. We had made fun of their Siegfried Line - a line of gun emplacements and trenches and barbed wire - meant to keep an invading army out of Germany. And of course, we thought the Siegfried Line was a very poor imitation of the French defensive line - the Maginot Line. No one could ever break through the French one, and it was just a matter of time before Hitler was on his knees. We were so confident of this there was a popular song we all sang:

> "We're going to hang out the washing on the Siegfried Line,
> Have you any dirty washing, Mother dear,
> We're gonna hang out the washing on the Siegfried Line,
> 'cause the washing day is here...
>
> Whether the weather may be wet or fine
> We'll just rub along without a care
> We're going to hang out the washing on the Siegfried Line
> If the Siegfried Line's still there."

In the spring of 1940, that song showed how confident we were about beating the Jerries. But early that summer, the Jerries sprang into action, and in no time, they were advancing everywhere - in Norway, through Belgium and Holland and France, and the song about the Siegfried Line was forgotten. Far from looking like an easy victory for Britain and France, it was becoming a desperate struggle to survive. The War was becoming serious. We couldn't afford jokes about the LDV. More German planes were attacking the convoys and they were bombing other places though Peterhead had a charmed existence. We had lots of Air Raid Warnings, but never an attack on the town.

And we became Spy Conscious. That "Careless Talk" poster meant something now. Were there spies in Peterhead? Well, one Saturday afternoon a group of us bairns from the Blinner discovered a couple of spies. And here's how it happened and what we did about it.

You could tell they were spies, because they were men dressed up as wifies. And we knew they were men because they were tall, they were striding it out and they seemed to be almost marching. We had never seen them before, they were not "Peterheid", so that left just one reasonable conclusion. They were spies. And if there was any doubt in our minds, then the fact they were walking along the Braes towards Buchanhaven, looking for places for Jerry invaders to land settled any possible doubt. So the bigger boys reached a decision, and that was to get the Bobbies. We did not tell our parents because - well, parents could be fooled and they did not have our imagination. So while the rest of us trailed the two "spies" at a distance, one of the older boys ran off to get the Bobbies. It wasn't long before he returned and said he'd told a Bobby - you always had Bobbies walking the beat in those days - so we decided to leave the spies to the law and we melted from the scene. Anyway, it was supper-time...

I wonder whatever happened to those two "spies". The more I think of it, the more I doubt the wisdom of our action, and in fact, from an adult point of view, I am bound to concede they were probably visitors to Peterhead, maybe to do with their husbands being stationed in the town with the forces. Did those two women wonder why a motley crowd of children were following them, and did they ever encounter the Police? Probably not, but in those spy-conscious days, you were ready to believe anything. Those were the days when stories were commonplace of spies betraying themselves by the daftest of actions, like a stranger going into a pub and asking for a double scotch, when everyone knew whisky was unobtainable, or another asking "Which town is this? And when is the next train to Glasgow?" when it was a village in the back of the beyond without a railway link.

It was probably in late spring the second wave of evacuees came from Glasgow and what we call the Central Belt nowadays. Peterhead was still a "safe area", and parents were still glad to get their children away from the cities to the comparative safety of Peterhead and other north-east towns and villages. It is true to say that most of the country villages were to be safe from enemy activity throughout the war, some hamlets never being bombed or machine-gunned. But that wasn't true for others.

The authorities were desperate to get homes for the children so we were asked to take two girls. I can't remember their names, but the older was about two years older than I, and the other was slightly younger. They would not have been my choice of evacuees, but they needed somewhere to live and my parents opened our house to them though I can't remember where they slept. Perhaps they had a "shakky-doon" in my sister's room - that is, a mattress on the floor, or maybe she slept on the "shakky-doon." What I can remember is that the older girl used to pee the bed and maybe that was because she was upset about leaving her family in Glasgow. Anyway, the evacuee lady gave mother a waterproof sheet and whatever else was needed to cope.

I have no idea what the girls did with their spare time because outside the house I can't remember playing with them. Perhaps they chummed up with the other girls in the street, or maybe they knew other evacuees. But in the house when it was raining or near bedtime they used to play "houses" beneath the living room table and on occasion I was persuaded to join them in their make-believe. That was a long time ago and I wonder if they remember their short stay in Peterhead, because it was a very short one. And I'll explain why.

On a Saturday, perhaps the first Saturday they were with us, or maybe it was the second, their mother and aunt came to visit them. It was a bonny afternoon when they arrived. I don't know where the grown-ups were going to sleep, or maybe they were going back to Glasgow the same evening, because buses and trains ran later in those days, or maybe they had a car though that would have been unusual, but I do remember they were having supper at our place, and the table was at the window. From our window we got a side-on view of the seashore, and we were having something like boiled ham and hard-boiled eggs and lettuce and maybe chips - that was the kind of thing you had for visitors - when an airplane roared low overhead. And then there was the most almighty "Bang!" and a huge column of water rose up in the air from the sea just down from the house. And almost simultaneously, the air-raid siren went.

"It's a Jerry!" father shouted. The women screamed, and father shepherded everyone into the lobby and made us lie down. He'd been in the trenches in the First World War and he knew about these things. My brother Alex, for a reason best known to himself, grabbed the cabinet clock off the sideboard and hugged it to him before he lay down beside us. It had been a brief visit from a Jerry bomber. We heard later it was being chased by a Spitfire, and jettisoned its bomb to help it escape. We never heard what happened to it, but we certainly heard its bomb. The All-Clear went and the emergency was over.

And it was all over for our girl evacuees, too. That evening, within an hour, they were on their way back to Glasgow. I've since wondered about the evacuees who lived with us. Did they survive the war, because I know Glasgow and Clydebank got badly bombed later on by the Germans? If they did survive the war, I'm confident they would never forget their first encounter with a German bomb, the one that landed doon the Braes.

Chapter 5

Flotsam from War

1940 was a lovely spring and summer. We were just emerging from the Phoney War, and we'd had our bomb at the Gadle Braes. It never made the pages of the *Buchanie* because nothing really happened apart from the scare. The Jerry bomber was chased out to sea by a Spitfire and I never heard if the bomber was shot down. On the horizon we could see convoys being bombed. The press carried a warning against taking photographs in sensitive areas. In fact, you had to ask permission to take photographs of the harbour and most places which could be of "military importance", and that covered just about everywhere including empty fields and the foreshore - both of which could be landing sites for Jerry invaders. So if you wanted to take a photo of someone at the Braes, you had to get permission. But since I don't remember the Davidsons owning a camera, it didn't affect us.

The Local Defence Volunteers were issued with their anti-invasion kit, an ancient Lee-Enfield rifle and a blanket. And so they would spend nights guarding our coastline. One of their places was the boating pond near the Lido, and my future brother-in-law, Sandy Watson, as a seventeen-year old, remembered wrapping himself in his LDV blanket and lying beside the Pond and peering out to sea, his rifle at the ready. By morning he and his fellow-LDV would be soaked with dew. Then they went home for breakfast before going to work. But everyone was in a state of readiness for the German invasion because Hitler and his gang were winning everywhere on the Continent and it seemed a matter of time before he chanced his luck against us.

The newspapers gave us advice on how to prepare for "a bombardment from the air". That was a quaint way of describing what came to be known as a "bombing raid". I never heard anyone call it "a bombardment from the air" but maybe that description was influenced by what the Luftwaffe did to places in Poland and Belgium when a bombardment from the air was perhaps an apt description. But the phrase never caught on with us. What we were advised to do was - in retrospect - as naive as the descriptive phrase: Householders were advised to keep a bath filled with water and empty the attic of anything that would burn. Perhaps the authorities were expecting the "bombardment from the air" to be with incendiary bombs and the biggest problem facing the civilian population would be fire. Many places did get heavy raids of incendiaries, especially cities like Clydebank, Coventry and London, but in Peterhead, our "bombardment from the air" was to be mostly with High Explosive bombs. That may have been because we had a harbour and often the targets were not warehouses and factories, but ships and installations at the quaysides, and incendiaries don't do much damage if they land on a concrete slip-way.

My father spent a large part of the war doing fire-watching night shifts after his day's work at the harbour, watching out for incendiary bombs, but I never heard of any incendiaries being dropped on Peterhead or the vicinity. Places such as public buildings and schools and shops were given stirrup pumps to fight fires. The stirrup pump is a wee pump which is placed against a bucket of water. One leg of the pump - the siphon bit - went into the water and you held the other leg down with your foot, and pumped a handle up and down like a bicycle pump. A thin jet of water scooted out of a hose and was supposed to extinguish the flames. I remember seeing it demonstrated on Ministry of Information films, but I don't think it would have done much good. Even as a bairn, I thought it looked a bit pathetic, with its wee jet of water. The water scooted a short distance, and it was only a bucketful of water. I thought it more sensible to throw the bucket of water straight on to the flames, and even better if it were a half dozen bucketsful.

Our two evacuee girls had returned to Glasgow, and mother reported their departure so we had a visit from the Evacuee Billeting wifey to arrange replacements. I can't remember what she was like, but those Billeting officers were chosen because they were real "battle-axes" and wouldn't take "No!" for an answer. Our next evacuees were three boys from the Gorbals area of Glasgow. I believe they had been placed with another family, but it didn't work out so they came to us. They arrived on a Sunday morning and they were the Sharp boys. Archie who would have been about 13 and Robert, a frail round shouldered boy about 11 and Josie, a bit younger than myself. And from the very beginning, we got on fine. There was no playing "hoosies" under the kitchen table with them.

Their outstanding possessions as I remember it were their **Dandy** and **Beano** books. Their supply of clothing was less impressive, and the Billeting woman gave mother a chit she took to the shops and bought heavy tweed coats and boots and whatever else they needed. I enjoyed having the Sharp boys living in the house though I can't remember where they slept. Probably in my sister's room and she used an armchair-cum-bed in the living room. It worked well, anyway, and there were no "bombardments from the air" to chase them back to Glasgow. Not yet, anyway.

Apart from being friendly boys, the outstanding thing about them was their haircuts. Their hair was cut close to the bone apart from a tuft right at the front. That seemed to be a fashion among the "glesga keelies" who were evacuated to Peterhead, and I think it was copied by some locals, though never by any of the boys from around the "Blinner". The Sharp boys blossomed in the fresh air of Peterhead and even Robert lost some of his frailty.

The summer of 1940 was lovely and sunny, but Peterhead became a gloomy town because the Jerries were winning in Europe. They conquered Holland and Belgium and Norway, and finally France, and lots of local soldiers were taken prisoner at a place called St Valery. I remembered that name because there was a song about it. I recall only snatches of it - something about "down by St Valery" and another line about the arrival "of the boys in blue", which I suppose meant the Royal Navy who helped by a flotilla of small private and civilian boats, evacuated thousands of our soldiers from Dunkirk. It may have included the RAF who fought against the Jerry bombers and fighters who were attacking our retreating BEF - which stood for British Expeditionary Force. Bairns knew all these names and what they stood for.

It was a bad time in the town and there wasn't much to smile about, especially since we were always hearing of someone either killed or wounded "at the front", or taken prisoner. People were raising money to send parcels to our boys in German prisoner of war camps, and some of the Blinner boys decided to raise money, too. What we decided was to make wooden models of aircraft, paint them to look real, and then sell them, and the money would go for POW (Prisoner of War) parcels via the Red Cross. I was too young to wield a knife for "fiting the wid" - whittling the wood - but I could paint the finished article. And I could use my imagination, limited only by the paint available.

There was one plane I had painted and I really liked it. It was a German fighter and it was in the unlikely colour of white without camouflage, with crosses added on in bright red. I meant it as a Jerry fighter, though the colour scheme was not Luftwaffe, and it was more like a Red Cross plane, or maybe even a Swiss plane. Anyway, I pestered mother and she gave me twopence - a large sum in those days - so I could buy this beautiful plane I helped create. Looking back, I can't recall whatever happened to it.

Mother was asked to be treasurer of our POW relief charity. And the charity worked well for a few days. Then something went wrong - I have no idea what it was as I was not involved in important matters of policy, but it was decided after much weighty consideration, to disband the charity. We marched up the stairs to mother and she handed over the money we had raised, and it was shared out between us. So instead of our "boys over there" in the POW camps getting the fruit of labours, it was the Brig Shoppie (Shannies) who received our takings. We spent a half hour or so studying the halfpenny and penny trays to see how we could invest our money. That was the one and only effort I can remember of the boys from the Blinner raising money for charity though we did help with Backie Concerts later on.

Sirens were sounding more often now but still the bombing was confined to convoys of ships on the horizon. We could stand on the sea-front and see the tiny planes zooming over the convoys and occasionally the columns of spray thrown up by the bombs. British planes would head out from their airfields to fight off the Jerries and we would cheer them on their way. And mysterious white trails appeared in the skies over Peterhad and way out to sea. We boys recognised this was a secret weapon. A newspaper had an article by an expert who pretended these white trails were simply condensation trails from planes. Nonsense! We were not fooled. We had never seen anything like it before, and to say it was just vapour trails did not ring true. It was a British secret weapon, and it would beat the Jerries and Hitler was going to be sorry he ever started anything with us. And in fact, it is still possible to see that "secret weapon" when high-flying planes go overhead...Another secret weapon was a tunnel from Britain right under the sea to Berlin and it would blow everything up. But that idea lost credibility within weeks because some big boys said it was daft and they would know.

That summer we saw the convoys bombed, and unfortunately, not all the bombs were landing in the water. Some were hitting their targets, and ships were being sunk. We didn't actually see them sinking, but wreckage began washing up on the seafront, along the Salmon Nets and "ower the watter." And along with wreckage came some of their cargoes. There was the cargo of Canadian MacRed apples. I had never heard the name before, but within days, the whole town knew about Canadian MacReds, what they looked like, how they tasted, even though they were slightly salty. Boxes of them were washing up by Craigewan, and folk were collecting them, making their own personal caches, then arranging transport home. Bonny shiny red apples half-filled our bath. I can't remember why they were in the bath, but mother probably washed them in it, then the apples were polished and passed by hand along a human chain for storage in the scullery.

We had stewed apples, individual apples in a pastry jacket, apple pie, apple crumble, apple tarts, and we even ate raw apples. Most children were eating an apple on the way to school, and we feasted on them because there was no way to keep them - there was no such thing as refrigerators in those days, not in ordinary people's houses. So for a few weeks, the people of Peterhead dined well on apples.

Then there were sardines. Boxes of tins of sardines floated in from the sea. And they could be stored indefinitely, so there was no need to eat them up in a short time. The town was awash with sardines. It was then I first learned the joy of sardines on toast. I remember seeing a grocer shop in town with a pile of sardine tins in the window and they were for sale. But how could anyone hope to sell sardines when they were lying along the beach for picking up. Or was the grocer selling sardines from the beach? Was that legal? Anyway, I have no idea if he sold any of his sardines, but I know we had all the sardines we could cope with. Strangely enough, it never occurred to bairns what suffering was involved in those apples and sardines being washed up on our beaches, though I'm sure our parents had their thoughts.

Some time about this period of the war, probably in the autumn of 1940, lard was washed up on the beach. They came in barrels, but in many instances, the barrel-staves had broken off and what washed up were great big lumps of what looked like white fat. So the folk of Peterhead went beach-combing for lard. Our oldest evacuee, Archie Sharp, disappeared one afternoon as soon as he came home from school, going off on his own. He was away for an hour or two and mother was getting worried about his non-appearance. Then about six o'clock, Archie reappeared.

"Mrs Davidson, Mrs Davidson - Look!" he announced triumphantly.

Mother about fainted. Archie, resplendent in his bonny new boots and tweedy belted coat, was clasping a huge lump of fat to his chest. He had carried it thus all the way from the "Salmon Nets". But when he tried to lower the lard to the floor, it stuck to him. It had to be prised off his coat. What a bonny lump of lard, but what a mess of a coat. It was no longer new, and I have no idea how mother cleaned it, but she managed to restore it to some degree of normality, though obviously not so bonny as it was before. And the lard? Well, Archie meant well, and mother was grateful for his thoughtfulness. So she used the lard to make chips and pastry for sausage rolls. She made lovely flaky pastry, and I can still recall the taste of those chips and sausage rolls. The only thing was your mouth felt sticky afterwards. But what of that, the chips and sausage rolls tasted good.

And then the stickiness was explained when an announcement in the paper a few days later said it wasn't lard being washing up on our beaches, but tallow for candle-making. But it looked like lard, and since we had never seen so much lard before, no one could be blamed for the mistake. Anyway, it didn't do us any harm.

Later in the war, motor-bikes in wooden crates were said to be washing up on the beach over towards Rattray Head but I never heard of anyone who actually found one, and it may not have been true. But then again, if motor-bikes were washing up, I doubt if the authorities would have allowed beach-combing for such valuable flotsam. Apples and sardines and tallow is one thing, but motor-bikes is a different matter altogether. But would motor-bikes have washed in on the tide, even if they were in wooden crates. Would they have floated? I have my doubts. And then again, all the beaches and dunes over by Craigewan and Rattray were eventually sown with mines and surrounded with barbed-wire, so beach-combing over there would have been forbidden, and downright dangerous for anyone who risked it. I can't remember any more cargo from bombed ships coming ashore at Peterhead, though there was to be more flotsam, later in the war, and nearer home than Craigewan. In fact, it came from vessels grounded in the Bay and their discharged coal washed up on the foreshore at the Lido and near Crosse & Blackwell's.

Chapter 6

"Careless Talk Costs Lives"

In the war years, only one side of the "first streetie", the road from the sea front up to Ugie Road dividing Ives Park from Ugie Park, had been completed. The Ugie Park side had fenced gardens up to the back gardens of houses on Ugie Road, but on the Ives Park side, there was only one block of houses above the "Blinner" then after that, an expanse of waste ground covered with rough grass and nettles and dockin leaves. That rough ground was all the way up to the "Briggie" that carried Ugie Road over the railway line.

You couldn't play on the rough ground. It was too overgrown and pitted with holes, and if you wanted to play fitba, then it had to be the Blinner, or up the road to Raemoss and the swing-park. So, naturally, there was a great deal of interest among the bairns when soldiers arrived and started work on that piece of rough ground. It took about two days for them to complete their work, but when they left, there was their handiwork for all to see. The rough area now had three small trenches running parallel to Ugie Road with their parapet edges facing towards the houses. And there were coils of barbed wire between them and the houses, as an added protection against an invading army landing down the Gadle Braes. Up beside Ugie Road, they had erected a wooden framed machine-gun post, covered with sandbags. It had a narrow doorway facing on to the railway line, and there were narrow slit-windows facing in all four directions. On the sandbagged roof were more coils of barbed wire. It looked very smart though one mortar shell would have pulverised it.

So we witnessed the anti-invasion defences being built around Peterhead. A concrete machine-gun post with walls about two feet thick was sited along the Braes from our house, about half way from the bottom of the "first streetie" and the end of Ives Park towards the "cable hoosie" right at the top of the cliff. I had better explain: Ives Park had three blocks of council houses facing on to the sea, then there was a gap between Ives Park and the Roanheads. About a hundred yards from Ives Park towards the Roanheads was the "cable hoosie", which was the ter-

There is another concrete shelter - near the Craigewan rocks "ower the watter -"

minus building for an underground telegraph cable which stretched across under the North Sea to Norway. The story was that news of the Russian Revolution of November, 1917, came to Britain through our "cable hoosie". After the "cable hoosie" was a stretch of grassy braes with a footpath running alongside the railway track to what is now the junction of North Street and East North Street, and here a rail spur went in to the "killin hoose" - the abattoir - and the main line went on to the terminus and coal depot at the Roanheads, just to the north of the slipway.

Along by the railway line between the "cable hoosie" and the "killing hoose" on the Wilson Road was a high granite wall which separated fish yards and the JIC from the railway line. The JIC was the Junior Instruction Centre, an education centre for unemployed teenagers before the War. But the JIC fell into disuse when the unemployed went off to serve their King and Country.

In 1940, the Army were stationed in it, and when you passed on Wilson Road you could see guns and Bren-gun carriers parked in its quadrangle. The barrels of anti-aircraft guns - they were two bofor quick-fire guns and I think a heavy machine-gun - poked over the wall and pointed out to sea, all part of the anti-invasion defences built in and around Peterhead that summer of 1940 when Britain and her empire stood against Hitler and his all-conquering armies. Like the rest of the country, Peterhead was getting ready to fulfil Winston Churchill's promise in early June:

"We shall fight on the beaches, we shall fight in the fields ... we shall never surrender."

There was another machine-gun emplacement just like the one at the top of our road out in a field beside the narrow "shunner roadie" out to Inverugie Station, about half way to the "fower pluntins" - or "four plantations", a wooded crossroads. Those defences were dismantled a long time ago, though you can see a fragment of concrete sticking above the grass of the one built beside Ives Park. There is another concrete shelter, partly on its side near the Craigewan rocks, "ower the Watter". And while there were causey blocks, big rectangular blocks of reinforced concrete, springing up all over the place designed to block enemy tanks - there are still some of them on the river estuary at Cruden Bay - those most important to us were at the foot of our road. They went from the pavement along the Gadle Braes down to the dike which overlooked the beach, almost midway between the bottoms of the "first streetie" and the "second streetie", or as we know them today, Ives Road and Raemoss Road.

Recently I saw the German's Atlantic Wall near Bordeaux on the French Atlantic Coast, and Peterhead's defences were puny by comparison. But at the time we thought they were pretty good, though we bairns felt they could be improved on. So we determined to give the "sojers" a help and dig another trench. Our trench would be nearer the sea than the ones on the rough ground at the top of the road. It would be on a patch of ground between the Cameron's and the Ritchie's garden, and it would have a clear view of the sea, ideally positioned to repel invaders who dared to land below our houses.

The Cameron and Ritchie boys were involved in digging this trench because it was in their gardens. But all the Blinner boys were in it, too, though the younger ones like myself were watchers rather than diggers. The hole in the ground went deeper as spade and garden fork and pick-axe went to work, wielded by willing twelve and thirteen year olds. Down below the top-soil into the clay, then the sand, the trench went.

Then disaster! Water flooded the hole. Where had it come from? There was panic and the thought - "we've burst a water pipe". Or could it be a sewer pipe? We convinced ourselves it was an underground spring. But we didn't wait to verify this. The earth was thrown back in, and a vow of silence agreed. It was only when writing these memories that I remembered that water in the trench, and it never occurred to me many years later - even when I was a member of the Council's Water Committee - to investigate what caused that inflow of water.

That was over sixty years ago and many of the diggers of the trench are no longer with us. So we should leave the mystery of the flooding trench, just as the Blinner boys did so long ago. Well, not quite, for we didn't abandon the idea of a trench altogether. Because there was still going to be an invasion and our sojers still needed our assistance. So another trench was dug, but farther up the brae and more into the Cameron and Ritchies' drying green, adjacent to the one for our house. This time, the trench went down and there was no water, just a satisfying hole in the ground, at least a foot deep. But once again, disaster struck.

Archie Sharp was swinging a garden fork into the ground and throwing earth and clay behind him. He worked like a trojan, "full butt", as we would say. You had to keep out of his way and let him tire himself out, before another boy could take over the digging. But Archie was into a rhythm, and the only thing for the rest of us was to watch. And to keep away from him - that was essential. Unfortunately, his brother, Robert, hadn't grasped that essential idea. And the fork tines speared once again into the ground. Sadly, it was the ground directly below Robert's new boot - the ones mother bought for him with a chit from the Billeting Lady - and Robert's foot was inside the boot.

The tine went right through the boot, through the foot, and into the ground. There was a howl - and for a brief paralysed moment, Robert could not move his foot because it was pinned to the ground. Then the fork was dragged out, and mother sent for. She arrived quickly and the damage was assessed. There was a hole right through the boot, and a blue hole through Robert's foot, though not much blood. Robert was taken to Dr Taylor who said that fortunately the tine had gone between the bones and there was no bad damage. I can't remember if he received injections, but he did limp for a wee while, though he never seemed much up nor down from his experience. However, that second mishap forced the Blinner lads to reconsider their defence project, and it was decided to leave trench digging to sojers!

I don't remember why the evacuees left Peterhead, but maybe it was because Peterhead was no longer designated "a safe area". Instead - as we all knew - it had become a possible landing spot for an invading German army. For whatever reason, Archie and Robert and Josie left us and returned to Glasgow. I think they were sorry to go, and I was sorry to lose them. They were good pals, and with them gone, so went most of the evacuees from the Central Belt, though there was still one or two Glasgow accents to be heard about Peterhead for years to come.

Longate bomb damage, Peterhead

It must have been soon after their departure that my mother took me with her to visit her half-sister, Auntie Cameron, in Gladstone Road. It was a pleasant summer's evening, or maybe early autumn. The air-raid alert siren went so we set off for home, though there was no hurry and no real alarm for us because we knew it wasn't Peterhead that was being raided but a convoy of ships on the horizon. We could see the Jerry planes swooping over the boats as we went along the road overlooking the rocks and the sea, with the railway line on our left.

Then we noticed that one of the Jerries - it had twin engines - had turned towards us and was heading for the coast. That scared us. It was coming for land, and though it was about ten miles away, we knew it wouldn't take long reach us. So we ran for Ives Park and safety. In the distance, coming for us, was father, and he was also running. The bofor guns over the wall in the JIC started firing, just above our heads, and they barked! and banged! and deafened us to run even faster. We met up with father about the Brookes' house, the last house in Ives Park and he hurried us into the small concrete bunker overlooking the cliff. From the safety of its windows we looked back, and saw that the Jerry plane had obviously changed its mind about coming after us - maybe the JIC guns had scared it off - for there was no sign of it. It must have gone back to attacking the ships because there was no sign of it being damaged or shot down either.

Each night, soldiers would mount guard at the foot of our road, sometimes standing in the shelter of the causey blocks, or along in the concrete emplacement we had taken refuge in. And my mother would take a tray of tea and something to eat down to them. I believe other women around that area did the same, probably organising it between themselves so that someone always provided for the soldiers on guard-duty. It seemed a natural thing to do and I suppose it was accepted by the powers-that-be, though when I myself was in the forces many years later I would have been in trouble if I were caught having tea and sandwiches while on guard duty. But in those days when we were expecting an invasion any time of the day or night, everyone was helping everyone else to do his duty as best we could. And a cup of tea and a home-made pancake and jam would fairly help a soldier keep alert during his lonely vigil.

It was always a highlight for us when a train pulling coal trucks or wagons of cattle came down the railway-line along by Ives Park. The engine would pull its load very slowly and make plenty of noise to let us know it was coming so as to warn anyone on the line to get out of the way. And of course, we did get out of the way, but not before laying half-pennies on the line in the fond hope they would be squashed bigger into pennies. One of the boys took his egg-shaped halfpenny up to the Brig

Shoppie to try to buy a penny's worth of sweets, but the old woman in the shop chased him away with a telling-off.

Sometime in July of 1940, the Jerries started to attack the north-east as well as the convoys off our coast, though there had been raids on Aberdeen for the past few months. In fact, there had been reports of people being killed in Aberdeen earlier in the year, but the worst raid yet was in July when about thirty bombs were dropped on Aberdeen. Most were in the harbour area and Hall Russell's shipyard was hit and more than thirty men were killed, including a fourteen-year-old boy, George Webster. In that raid, a Jerry bomber was shot down and there was a picture of it in the newspaper. If war had been an exciting game for us a few months earlier, it was deadly serious now.

Everyone was on invasion alert. It was all-out war and we had to be ready for anything. And we had to be especially alert for spies. "Careless Talk Costs Lives" - that's what the posters said, and Ministry of Information films were shown at the **Playhouse** and the **Regal** showing what could happen if you didn't watch your tongue.

A local retired business-man got into trouble that summer because he had been speaking on the phone to his daughter - I think she was in Edinburgh - about a bombing raid, and you were not supposed to speak about these things - "you never know who is listening!!" In fact, the telephone exchange operator must have been listening because he was reported to the police and he was charged with "careless talk" and when he came up before the sheriff, he was fined £5 and received a telling off. "No more careless talk!" There was a short propaganda film at the pictures about two girls in a railway-station waiting room speaking about their boy friends in the Royal Navy and how someone heard about a boat leaving for convoy duty, and the information got back to Hitler and a U-boat sank the boy-friend's ship. "Careless Talk Costs Lives!" That was good advice, and the Blinner boys took it to heart and there was no careless talk about our trench filling with water; not until now, that is.

Chapter 7

Backie Concerts and Bombs

A feature of the 1940 summer was the "backie concerts". A "backie concert" was a concert organised by the neighbours and held in one of their back gardens, or in the case of the folk round the Blinner, on the stairs going up to the Thom's and the McLean's front doors. It was in a large space between the two blocks of housing, and could easily hold over a hundred spectators, with the performers on the steps where everyone could see them. The purpose of those "backie concerts" was to raise money for our soldiers who were Prisoners of War. I have to say that Peterhead and district had an awful lot of men as PoWs, because so many of them had been in the 51st Highland Division, left behind at St Valery in France to keep the German soldiers busy while the remainder of the army got off at Dunkirk.

One of the Thom boys was a PoW, as well as a lot more soldiers from the town, so mothers held these "backie concerts", and organised raffles, with knitting and home baking as prizes. It was not uncommon to raise anything from £5 to £7 with a concert, which would have been a decent week's wages then, so the Red Cross were getting money in each week for PoW parcels. And of course, a favourite song was: "Down by St Valery", though the one I preferred was when a boy and a girl did a duet, singing about a little Dutch boy and a Dutch girl and the verse I can remember is when the girl sings:

> "Oh, go away, I hate you, I hate you, I hate you,
> Oh go away, I hate you, from over the sea."

Not hard to remember. However, the Dutch boy seemed to get round her in the end and they ended up best of pals in the final verse. There was another song in which a small boy in pyjamas sat on a woman's lap and she sang to him - I think it might have been: "Go to sleep, my little drummer boy..." A local man, Bobby Williamson, would tell jokes, and it didn't matter if you had heard them before, you always laughed. Bobby was a born comedian.

These "backie concerts" were held all over the town, and some artistes were in big demand. The two Freddie Duthies, father and son, used to do a musical turn, playing mouth organs. And there was a man Baird. And the woman Allison from Battery Park - she used to sing with the little boy in pyjamas on her lap. And though I didn't know it at the time, my future wife, Jeannie Wilson, a wee girl of five sang at these concerts though I can't remember hearing her. We would visit concerts in different parts of the town, and hear the same artistes do the same turns, and pay our pennies or whatever it was for admission fee. And the grown-ups would buy raffle tickets to win back the prizes they themselves had donated. So money was raised for the local loons in German prisoner-of-war camps. There was a great community spirit in those days and everyone helped because it was all for the war effort and for "our boys over there".

(Peterhead Academy 20/07/40) "In July two bombs were dropped on the town. One hit the Academy -"

The Jerry planes were coming more often, and not just to bomb convoys, but also to attack towns, especially Aberdeen. But Peterhead and the Broch were coming in for their share of bombing too. In July two bombs were dropped on the town. One hit the Academy, causing damage near the St Mary Street end, and another fell out by the second brig, landing in a field and killing some horses. It was not until August, 1940, however, before our town had people killed by the bombing.

Among the last people to get out of France ahead of the German army was a Peterhead woman, a Salvation Army officer, Mrs Major Golightly - her own name was Webster - who had been working along with her husband serving the troops in France. I suppose they had been working with the Red Shield, the SA's version of the NAAFI. She was reunited with her husband in London. There was also concern about a Strichen girl, a Miss Jean Scott who had graduated Honours in English from Aberdeen University and taken a job in a French university. She hadn't been heard of since before the Fall of France, and her relatives were worried that she may have fallen into the hands of the Germans - or worse. I wonder whatever happened to her.

Meanwhile, the north-east was being bombed, and an elderly couple - Mary and Thomas Ralph, and an eighteen-year-old girl, Mary Jane Herd, died in Fraserburgh in a raid in the second week of August. And a few days later, Peterhead suffered its first civilian deaths from German bombing.

On the 22nd August, bombs fell on the town and again badly damaged the Academy. Peterhead's first fatalities were at 68, York Street, where according to an eye-witness who lived nearby, it looked as if the whole roof and walls had caved in. The casualties were George Smith, a builder, and his five-year old grandson, Leslie Smith, and an ARP Warden, William Wyness from 61, Landale Road, who had taken shelter with the Smiths. Leslie's mother was injured in the bombing and a young friend, visiting them - I believe it was the Marioni girl - suffered from shock.

Not so long ago, a friend and neighbour, Mrs Belle Summers, told me how she worked for the Smiths, as a house maid, and she had just begun a big clean of their house. It was to be a two-days' task. She started the house-clean on the Thursday and was to complete it the next day, but the bomb fell on the house during the night, and she never finished the job. Her boss had been killed and part of the house demolished. Something I had not noticed before but was drawn to my attention recently by a Peterhead lady, Gwen Neish, was that during the autumn of 1940, raids on the town were usually restricted to a Tuesday and a Thursday. The Jerries may have been working a timetable, perhaps to leave their weekends free. Pupils were displaced from the Academy by the bombing, and were using part of the North School. Because of this, an appeal went out to parents of North School pupils for the use of parts of their homes, bedrooms or living rooms, as temporary classrooms.

Our house at 14 Ives Park became an Annexe of the North School, and one of our front bedrooms a classroom. It felt strange attending a school class, sitting in your own house on your own chairs though I think some were probably borrowed from neighbours. We would sit in a semi-circle a group of about ten pupils and our teacher writing on a blackboard propped up in front of the fireplace. We were all on our best behaviour and I wonder now just how much we learned or benefited because we had no desks to write on. But Miss Davidson, who was our teacher, managed fine. She had been a teacher of my parents and the rest of my family, and she was well-known and universally liked.

But father felt Peterhead was not a safe place, so he went off on his bike one Sunday out into the country, and when he returned in the evening, he had arranged for a Taylor family who had a farm and a joinery business out beside New Deer, to take mother and Alex and me in to stay with them as lodgers. And that was how I became an evacuee to the country. I enjoyed the country, and it must have involved missing school, because it was in the autumn, since I remember helping to stook the corn. On Sundays, Father would come and visit, and the other thing I remember about Sundays was that one of the Taylor boys would take me on the bar of his bike for a run through the woods. It was wild and fast, tearing along narrow paths and dodging tree stumps by inches.

Other Peterhead families, in fact neighbours from nearby, had moved out to farms in the New Deer area, and we sometimes visited them. I recall one day we had been invited over to one of the other houses for lunch - mince and tatties - and the two daughters of the house, both teenagers, were doing the cooking. Poor girls, they got their plans mixed up when it came to making the gravy for the mince, and they both salted it. Our dinner tasted like brine, and I remember someone telling the girls that the way to reduce the saltiness would have been to add a raw tatty to the gravy, as it would absorb surplus salt. I never forgot that culinary tip.

After a while on the farm, mother didn't like the thought of the family being split up so she insisted we return to Peterhead. Our rural evacuation came to an end and we went back to Peterhead by train from Maud station. I had forgotten that one of our front rooms was used as a classroom, and it was a shock to hear Miss Davidson's voice from the other side of the bedroom door. I tiptoed into the kitchen and kept quiet until she and the pupils had gone. But next morning, I reported to the classroom in our front bedroom. It was a strange experience using my sister's bedroom for classes, but it didn't last long, and after a few weeks we were back in proper classrooms in the North School.

It occurred to me only recently that I never heard people speak in those days of fighting the Nazis. We were fighting the Germans or the Jerries. Of course, we knew the Germans were a bad bunch, and I think it was in the *Sunday People* newspaper that I first read about the persecution of the Jews in Germany. There were articles about camps where the Jews were sent to be tortured and killed, though it was not until the end of the war that we discovered the full horror of the concentration camps - the Belsens and Dachaus. But during the war we did not differentiate between Nazis and Germans, they were all one to us and we were totally dedicated to fighting and defeating them.

There was always propaganda going on. Listening to the nine o'clock news was a sacred rite at the Davidson's house. And each news broadcast spoke of bombing raids on different parts of Britain and how many "enemy aircraft" had been shot down. But the numbers of civilian casualties continued to grow. The radio told us the Jerries were getting the worse of the exchanges. In fact, if all the Jerries claimed to be shot down had actually been shot down, the Luftwaffe would have run short of planes. But the Jerries were doing the same, and they claimed to have sunk more Royal Navy ships than we had when the war started.

And the newspapers spread propaganda all the time. An Aberdeen paper carried a tribute to the people of Peterhead "who have been having a very thin time." It was heady stuff, this anonymous citizen applauding us for our stiff upper lip, even though he could not go into details of our heroism in case he should face a firing squad - or so he said - for giving away secrets to the enemy. To quote from that long ago piece of propaganda: "Never in its long history has the capital of Buchan shown the white feather. You'll win through. Bless me, lads, you always do!"

Were our parents taken in by that? From today's perspective, I would say: "Of course not - it's blatant propaganda." But in those days, in the atmosphere of total war and almost daily air-raid alerts and awaiting an invasion at any time, yes, I could believe they were impressed by the admiration of that anonymous "John Citizen".

Conchies, or as they were officially known, Conscientious Objectors, were being hauled over the coals by a Tribunal, and there were a number of Conchies in Peterhead. Usually it was because of their religious beliefs. However, they did not get off without helping the war effort, because they could be drafted into the Medical Corps where they had a red cross on their uniforms and were not allowed to carry weapons. Others had to go away from home to work at certain industries or jobs essential to the war effort. But if they absolutely refused to do any of these duties, they went to prison. I don't know if any Peterhead men actually went to prison for their conscience, but it could have happened. At one tribunal, Shakespeare was quoted to conscientious objectors: "Conscience doth make cowards of us all," but I doubt if it had the desired effect. Shakespeare was not likely to change the mind of a Peterhead Conscientious Objector and make him go to war...if quoting the Bible couldn't.

A man appeared in the Sheriff Court in Aberdeen for the daftest crime imaginable. It seems he had been in town and managed to miss the last bus home so in order to get a bed for the night, he turned up at the Bridge of Don barracks and pretended to be a volunteer come to join the army. He got the bed, all right, but he was arrested when it was discovered next morning he was an imposter - no volunteer at all - and for his free bed from the Army, he got another thirty days and nights bed and full board as guests of HM the King.

That summer as we waited for the invasion, the public were told that if the Germans did come, we were to "stay put" - we had to remain in our homes. Otherwise fleeing refugees would block the roads as they did before the German army in Europe a few months previously, and then they would be an easy target for the Luftwaffe, as well as hindering the movement of our own soldiers.

And a new phrase was introduced in the press: "Shiver Sisters." A "Shiver Sister" was a woman who combined a faint heart with a vivid imagination, and she was always ready to believe the worst rumour and to spread it as gospel truth. "Shiver Sisters" were condemned as under-mining both morale and the war effort. So as we licked our wounds after the defeats on the Continent and prepared for the worst Hitler could throw at us in the autumn of 1940, what had been the Home Front prepared to become the Battle Front.

Part of this preparation for all-out war on the Home Front was that Italians who had been in Scotland living and working for many years, usually selling fish and chips or ice-cream, were now seen as possible spies or saboteurs, and were packed off to internment camps. I heard that a crowd of police would descend on the home of the Italians in the early hours of the morning and arrest them. At the time we had no idea where they went, but it came out later that many of them were interned on the Isle of Man, and I believe that my wife's father, Jimmy Wilson, who was in the soldiers met a Peterhead Italian in one of those internment camps. But that was in the future, and what I do remember is that everyone of German or Italian extraction was suspected of being an agent of Hitler. From today's perspective, that was ridiculous, but in those days of war hysteria, anything was possible. And of course we had local people being killed by the Jerries and the town being bombed, so it was better to be safe than sorry.

Chapter 8

Invasion fears

That autumn in 1940, invasion fears were uppermost in all our minds. The town was full of soldiers and the RAF patrolled the skies, and the nights were spent mostly in shelters of one kind or another, as Jerry planes flew overhead, usually on their way to somewhere else. Father tried various shelters for us. We even went with a neighbouring family to spend a night in the concrete emplacement along the top of the braes from our house, but it wasn't comfortable. Then we decided on the cupboard space in our downstairs neighbours' beneath the stairs up to our house. It would give a little shelter - better than under the table or the bed anyway - and somehow we and the Hamiltons fitted into that crowded space. It would never withstand a direct hit, but nothing would. Not even a concrete and granite shelter. But as the darker nights of 1940 drew in, we waited for whatever Adolf and his gang threw at us.

There weren't many funny experiences from the wartime, but one I remember well happened during a bombing raid, when we were all cramped into that space under the stairs in the Hamilton's house. Our lighting was primitive, small torch bulbs lit by a wet battery from a wireless. The Jerries were overhead and we could hear their whistling bombs - it was all right if you heard them whistling because that meant they had passed over you going somewhere else - and the heavy thumps of explosions, and the ground occasionally shaking. Our lighting had failed and we were plunged into darkness, and there was an almighty bang from nearby, probably from the bomb which landed in the tarmac tennis court beside Victoria Road.

The house shook and my mother cried out: "I've swallowed my teeth." She had dentures, top and bottom, and swallowing her teeth was cause indeed for alarm. Then when the light was restored, there were the false teeth, lying in her lap. Big laugh all round, and eventually the Jerries went away, the All Clear sounded, and we could go back to our beds, still smiling over the "swallowed" teeth. But it just shows the jarring we all felt when that bomb fell on the tarmac. When bombs landed on soft earth it didn't shake you nearly so much.

I was taught to pray before I fell asleep - "This night while I lie down to sleep, I pray the Lord my soul to keep, if I should die before I wake, I pray the Lord my soul to take - God bless so and so, etc." During those nights of bombs and the possibility of being blown to pieces, I suppose the prayer about dying before I woke had an added significance. But in addition to wounding and killing, there were other kinds of injuries that bombs could do. It was the following afternoon when I came home from school that mother asked me: "Fits wrang wi' yer face?" My only reply could be: "Nithing!" But she wasn't satisfied, and when they came home from work, father and Jess were asked for their opinion about my face, and they agreed there was something wrong with it. So I was taken to Dr Taylor's, and he decided there might be something wrong with my face after all. "Fit ye bothering wi' my face, for?" I complained, because I was too young to worry about how I looked.

And while I was not aware of anything wrong with me, others could see that my mouth was twisting up to one side. Doctor Taylor suggested a visit to Mr Craig the dentist to get a big tooth at the back extracted and that might straighten my face. So off we went to Chapel Street to see Mr Craig, who obliged and pulled a big one at the back which might be causing the problem. But the next afternoon after school, my face was no better. So we returned to Dr Taylor's, and this time he decided I should go to Woolmanhill Hospital in Aberdeen for examination. A few days later, mother and I took the bus to Aberdeen, and I was scared stiff I would be kept in hospital among a lot of strangers. My first stay in hospital had been pleasant enough, but not an experience I wanted to repeat. But the doctors of Woolmanhill had no intention of putting me in one of their beds. Instead, they twisted a piece of rubber covered wire with one end fitted into my mouth and the other looped round my ear, to pull my mouth back to a normal shape. Hardly the height of modern technology.

As a treat, mother took me into a small cafe which jutted out from the bridge over the railway just up from Woolmanhill where people looked at my face with its rubberised brace, and I discovered it attracted attention, even sympathy. I had been diagnosed as having Facial Paralysis, probably caused by the shock of the bombs. In fact, I was a war casualty. And I enjoyed the fame it conferred on me. When other bairns asked what was wrong I proudly answered: "The Jerries did it." And so they had, though I've wondered since how many other bairns around the world have suffered from enemy action, and how many others had Facial Paralysis and a lot worse, like the wee girl in Vietnam running down the road greetin with her skin burned off with napalm. Facial Paralysis indeed. The only inconvenience was the taste of the rubber and strangely enough, I can still feel the grating of the wire on my teeth. Because, of course, I had to chew the rubber off...

Mother visited a lady she knew in Aberdeen. I think she lived in a flat above a shop in George Street, and I remember two things about that visit. One was the model of a Spitfire made by her son in the RAF from a piece of aluminium. The other was her telling us she saw the crew of a German U-boat being marched up George Street, on their way to a prisoner-of-war camp. I wasn't all that interested in the story of the German sailors, but I coveted that Spitfire. It must still be around somewhere, someone's family heirloom, no doubt. A few weeks later Doctor Taylor said my mouth was better and I could throw away the brace. I took him at his word and threw it into the front garden of a house in Queen Street, a house which was later bombed.

That was a long hot August in 1940, and it was the month of what became known as the Battle of Britain. The nine o'clock news gave the numbers of enemy aircraft shot down. After the war we learned these numbers had been exaggerated by double. Truth is one of the first casualties in a war.

The fact is, however, we were shooting down almost two or three Jerries for every Spitfire or Hurricane shot down. Unfortunately, we had started the war with many fewer planes than Hitler, so even at three of them for one us, we could still lose. The sirens kept sounding at night, and occasionally bombs were dropped on or around Peterhead. Underneath the staircase was judged to be all right for "a shove away", a temporary emergency shelter, but we needed something roomier and even safer. So we moved down into the "foons" - the foundations of the block... below the floor boards.

Since we were on a brae, and we and the Hamiltons were higher up the brae, and the Camerons and the Ritchies more down the brae, it was recognised that the "foons" at their end of the block would have more head room than our end. So it was when the siren went at night, we all trooped into the Camerons' and down through a trap door in their lobby floor and into their "foons". Each family had a space down there, and we had mattresses and blankets and a lighting system fixed up and it was safe from everything except a direct hit. We were below ground level and reasonably comfortable, though I grew to detest the damp "mochty" smell, and was always glad of a night spent in my own bed rather than under the floor-boards.

The Jerries were bombing London every night now, and it was a great satisfaction for us to hear one night on the news that the RAF had bombed Berlin. And it wasn't propaganda, it had really happened, and later we were to hear that Hitler was "fizzing" at Goering because Goering had promised that Berlin would never have a bomb dropped on it. Before the war ended, that boast of Goering would be thrown back in his teeth many thousand-fold.

We bairns were singing a rather rude song at this time, though I confess I wasn't old enough to understand what it meant, though wise enough not to let my parents hear it. It was a song about the apparent physical inadequacy of Hitler and Goering and Himmler and Goebels to father children. In fact the closing line actually rhymed with Goebels' name, and since he and his wife had a number of children - they killed their daughters at the end of the war before committing suicide themselves - the song was obviously inaccurate in describing that gentleman's impotency. At the time, when we were suffering from German air-raids, we would have rejoiced in the thought of Goebels and family dying at their own hands, though the passage of time and more mature consideration simply leaves me sad for parents who felt they had to poison their children before committing suicide. War is a form of collective madness, a natural fault in mankind taken to its extremity.

But in August, 1940, with the press and wireless continually urging us to be ready for an invasion by the Huns, a red mist had fallen over the eyes of the British people, and we were determined to fight like our hero, Winston Churchill, had said earlier that summer: "We shall fight on the beaches, we shall fight ..etc." We were determined to fight. And it was about this time that the LDV were given khaki denim uniforms and renamed The Home Guard. And now, the Home Guards were no figure of fun. "Dad's Army" is a comedy series, but the Home Guard in the autumn of 1940 were no joke. They were serious, and they looked "just like real sojers". And they were ready for the invasion. In fact we were all ready, even if it meant fighting with our bare hands, and unfortunately, if the Jerries had come to Peterhead that August, it could well have ended up with bare hands because we didn't have much else to fight with. Most of our Army's equipment had been left on the beaches at Dunkirk.

A soldier appeared in Peterhead Sheriff Court for a rather daft offence. Apparently one of the Home Guard had taken his rifle with him to a dance in St Fergus, and the soldier wanted to demonstrate how to use the rifle. Of course, there were admiring females watching it all, so the soldier went through the drill, pointed the rifle at the roof, and since the rifle had no bullet in it, he pulled the trigger. Unfortunately, there was a bullet up the spout, the rifle went off, and it blew a hole in the roof.

The sheriff gave the soldier a right dressing down, and as for the Home Guard member who had brought a loaded rifle to a dance, he was left to the tender mercy of his commanding officer. But it just shows there was a feeling of impending invasion that a Home Guard man carried a loaded rifle around with him, even to a dance. Fairly recently, an elderly gentleman came to see me because he wanted to tell me in detail about that incident, and how it happened was thus:

He was a private in the Home Guard, and he and another private, along with the corporal, went to look in by the dance because they were on duty that night on the bents east of St Fergus, and a wee while in the dance wouldn't do any harm. Now the privates were not allowed to carry bullets about with them, the corporal was in charge of ordnance, and it was his responsibility to dish it out if the Jerries invaded. However, since he had the bullets, he decided to put a clip in his own rifle, and it was on his rifle the soldier demonstrated his prowess. Well, after the rifle went off, the three Home Guards rapidly vacated the premises and once outside they met a policeman who was investigating the noise.

To the policeman's inquiry about what made the noise, my informant replied: "It must hae been a car back-fire!" and the policeman whose name escapes me, though the adjective "Inquisitive" could well figure in it, agreed - it probably was "a car back-fire", though all four knew St Fergus didn't boast a car. Anyway, the three Home Guards went across the bents on their patrol and returned to the dance-hall for a bit of fun at closing time. My informant told me about it: "'Halt, who goes there?" we demanded of everyone coming out of the dance, and the quines said: 'dinna be daft. Ye ken me.' We had richt fun that nicht," he chuckled.

Frequently, people appeared in court for letting a light show from their houses, though this became more serious as we moved into late autumn and the darker nights. A New Deer woman was fined fifteen shillings (75 pence in today's money) - for showing a light from her children's bedroom. The two blankets she had hung up to block the light had proved inadequate, and the Sheriff advised her that she ought to get her children accustomed to the dark for their own safety, as well as for her duty to the public. So wherever you lived, in city, town or country, the blackout restrictions applied and as winter came on with the darker nights, it was more important than ever that you never showed a chink of light from your property after dark.

The thing is that bombs would sometimes land in the country, even in open fields, as in the case of the horses killed in July beside the second brig. There was another occasion when farm workers transporting a threshing mill had to throw themselves under the mill to shelter when bombs and incendiaries fell in nearby fields. I suspect, however, that these bombings were when German bombers returning from distant targets simply dropped what was in their bomb-bays rather than try to land back in Norway with bombs still on board. There was the occasional story about how Jerries would rather drop bombs on open countryside than on a town, but I suspect that was a false story spread by Lord Haw Haw, the English traitor who worked for Hitler. His real name was William Joyce.

We could all impersonate Lord Haw-Haw. "Germany calling, Germany calling," he would say in his posh nasal accent. "Are the people of Peterhead getting a good night's sleep these nights? Well, if you aren't, you can blame that warmonger, Winston Churchill...etc" That was the kind of propaganda he poured out on the radio and sometimes we listened to him to see if he mentioned our town, but he didn't make any converts. He was on a loser, and he was to get his just desserts, all in good time.

Mother had written to my brother, Willum, telling him that most nights we were going down to the shelter, though she had not explained just where the shelter was. That led to an amusing experience when Willum came home on leave one night. He arrived in a blacked out Peterhead, with an air-raid going on though I don't think any bombs had actually landed in the town. Anyway, since he couldn't get into our house, he went about the garden on his hands and knees in the pitch dark, feeling about for the Anderson shelter. And of course, he couldn't find it. There wasn't one.

Then the back door of the Cameron's house opened and Kikes Cameron, man of the house, looked out and called: "Fa's at?" to which my brother identified himself, saying he was looking for the shelter where his family were. "They're in here - doon in the foon," explained Kikes, and so it was that Willum arrived in our midst beneath the floor boards, and I felt a lot more secure with my soldier hero armed with rifle and bayonet and bullets keeping me company. I slept a bit more soundly on my makeshift bed "doon in the foons".

There weren't many Anderson shelters in Peterhead, the kind of shelter Willum had been looking for, a hole in the garden with a corrugated iron roof bent over it and surrounded by sand-bags. Apparently you needed planning permission from the Council to build one. So nothing has changed. Under the circumstances, in our granite-built house with us well below the level of the ground, we were probably safer than if we had been in Anderson shelters. But it was all the same where you were if you received a direct hit. Council houses had a back-bedroom on the ground floor with a brick L-shaped wall built outside the window to protect the interior from blast. I don't know how effective the blast-wall would have been, but they lasted the war out. As the winter of 1940 drew on, the subject of getting a good safe shelter exercised the minds of

"There weren't many Anderson shelters in Peterhead -"

adults, while the bairns were aware of their concern, and the pleasurable excitement of War had long since gone.

Chapter 9

Casualties and Censorship

Of the 1,075 civilians killed by enemy action in Britain during August, 1940, one was in Aberdeen, three in the Broch, and three in Peterhead. But the Broch was to get a real baptism in fire later that year. That summer, the *Fraserburgh Herald* had complained it was a dirty trick by the Jerries to drop two bombs on the town's bowling green. And a few weeks later, the newspaper had a marvellous understatement when it gave as the reason for the bowling club's finals and "hat night" tournament being switched to the East Links rinks that there had been some damage to the turf. "Damage" indeed - two bombs worth of damage. The *Herald* was even more coy in dealing with what the Jerries did on the following Guy Fawkes night, when the Broch was to suffer the deaths of more than fifty people from another two bombs! The local paper made no specific reference to that tragedy...

For civilians, War meant the possibility of sudden death from the sky without warning, especially in the dark when it was possible for a German plane to sneak over without detection. If the Air-raid Siren went, then you could take shelter, but sheltering under the bed or the stairways or down in the foundations or cellars of a building can be a frightening experience when bombs are falling. You never know when the next moment will be your last, and it is amazing how people deal with it. We adopted various strategies for coping with danger. My wife's family and all their neighbours who lived in Love Lane sheltered in their cellar - they named it "the dungeon" - and sang to keep their spirits up. It must have been a popular meeting place for during a raid they were sometimes joined by patrons from the nearby **Regal**. In another family, the mother had a bag of barley sugar she handed round because the crunching of teeth was even louder than the explosions. Or so her daughter told me. In the "foons" beneath the Cameron's floor-boards, we had no particular way of distracting ourselves from the noise of war, though I expect some of us prayed. I remember my brother, Willum, saying that in a particularly bad few weeks in 1944, pinned down by German counter-attacks near Caen in Normandy, a number of his mates were praying, even those who said they didn't believe in God. There's a saying: "There's no such thing as an atheist in a trench." It could be true. It was said that even Germans prayed, though we were sure God wouldn't listen to them. But it does show that God becomes important when you think you could be killed soon.

And death came to many civilians when it was farthest from their thoughts. That's how it was for many in Fraserburgh on the evening of Tuesday, 5th November, 1940 - Guy Fawkes night. There was a fire in a big department store - Benzie and Miller's. In addition to selling furniture, B & M's was well-known for its selection of fashion clothing, and its popular tea-room.The Jerries seemed to have got into the habit of coming over on a Tuesday and a Thursday, and this Tuesday they were attracted by the B&M fire glowing for miles in the dark. They must have seen it halfway from Norway. Unfortunately, a crowd had gathered to see the fire. Nearby was a public-house where a darts tournament was in progress and it also had a crowd of spectators and competitors. So when the Jerries came over, there were hundreds of people in the target area.

The local paper did not mention that bombing. In fact, the *Fraserburgh Herald* did not appear for two weeks, but that was probably because their premises had been damaged in the raid. It did appear again on the 26th November, but there was no direct reference to the bombing or casualties. Instead, the editor used a ploy to get round the censorship. On the back page appeared a long and descriptive essay by a boy from the local academy, a six-year pupil named George May. The composition was headed: "Fire in the North East", and it didn't say where the fire had been because it was supposed to be a piece of imaginative writing by a schoolboy. As a schoolboy's composition, it passed the censor, though in fact it was an eye-witness description of the Guy Fawkes bombing.

George May had been on fire-watching duties along with other friends the night a fire broke out in Benzie and Miller's. He described beams twisting with heat, and furniture going up in gouts of sparks and flame. The locals gathered to see the spectacle and kept pressing forwards at both ends of the short street despite the attempts by soldiers to keep them well back. The heat must have been intense since the roofs of buildings up to a hundred yards from the blaze were doused with water by the Fire Service. The whole place was threatening to go up in flames.

George and those with him had to transfer important documents and other material from a nearby bank - it was the Clydesdale - which was threatened by fire - to a safer neighbouring premises, while the flames and sparks shot high into the darkness above. Suddenly, there was a loud screeching sound, and George and his companions threw themselves to the ground. Immediately, there followed two loud explosions. It was bombs exploding. George remembered the sight of the bodies of dead and injured being pulled from the wreckage. It obviously had a traumatic effect on the schoolboy, and he ended his essay asking why it was that human beings could do this to their fellow men. Why indeed!

The schoolboy made no attempt to identify the site of the fire or the bombing, or even if it was a real event or a flight of fancy, but there is no doubt that George May was describing the worst night of the war for the Broch. After the bombing, the *Herald* did not appear until 26th November, when in addition to publishing George's composition, it gave a further clue to the bombing disaster. The Fraserburgh cinema, the **Picture House**, across the street from B&M's, had its usual advert space blank apart from an announcement that the cinema was closed for repairs until further notice. It appeared to have been damaged in the raid, as had Marioni's Restaurant and Billiard Saloon with its twelve full-size tables.

Twenty-two civilians were killed in that bombing raid. Among the dead were a Rosehearty couple in their twenties who had been married only seven months, James and Jessie Cruickshank, and a five-years old girl, Edith Glennie. The war had come to the Broch with a vengeance. But what I found out many years later was that apart from the civilian casualties, thirty-six Royal Scots soldiers were killed when the Jerries scored a direct hit on the Commercial Bar. Woolworths of today stands on the site of the Comercial. That makes fifty-eight deaths, apart from the many injured.

The Guy Fawkes' night bombing gave an ironic twist to what had appeared in local newspapers a few weeks previously. It was a piece of propaganda from the Civil Defence, pointing out that 5,000 people were killed and 200,000 injured on the roads every year. It went on to say that while the ARP could not prevent air-raids, it could make the prospect of surviving an air-raid even greater than the chance of safely crossing a main trunk road on a Bank Holiday. It ended on an encouraging note: "Take heart from the knowledge that the odds are several thousand to one against your being hurt by a bomb." Two bombs and fifty-eight killed in one raid on Fraserburgh on Guy Fawkes' Night, 1940, didn't sit easily with those odds.

Everyone was talking about an invasion. As bairns we scanned the horizon for Jerry warships but they never came. There was a series in *The Sunday Post* about how the Jerries invaded Scotland - I think they landed in Fife - and I read it every week until the invaders were eventually thrown back into the North Sea. Hooray! Even the Sunday paper said we could beat the Jerries, and during the weeks of that series, I enjoyed that page even more than the Fun Section with *Oor Wullie* and *The Broons*. A few years ago I was invited to see drawings on the walls of a cupboard in Duff House in Banff where German PoWs had been locked up during the war. Apparently an officer of the Wermacht had still dreamed of an invasion because he drew a map of north-east Scotland on which he laid out the battle-plan of the Allied defenders and the invading Germans and showed how his side could win. But that must have been a forlorn hope for him because apparently he was taken prisoner in North Africa when the Allies were winning battles and the possibility of a German invasion had receded to zero. But it is interesting to compare photographs of that wishful thinking of the German officer and my memories of the invasion series in *The Sunday Post*. They had a lot in common in addition to being pure fiction.

In late 1940, we bairns prepared for war. We drilled and marched and waited for those Jerry ships to appear over the horizon. That is why we started our parachute brigade. We had one parachute. It wasn't a real parachute; it was a large table-cloth, discarded by one of our mothers, and round its edges at regular intervals we tied lengths of rope. The loose ends of the ropes were joined together, and that was our 'chute. If you wanted to be a paratroop, you had to do a proper parachute jump with it. What that involved was climbing on to the causey block at the foot of the grassy bank, just above the chingly beach doon the braes from what is now Ives Road and Raemoss Road. That site is gone now, but it's fresh in my mind's eye. The would-be paratrooper had to hold on to the loose ends of the ropes and jump about a ten-foot drop on to the chingle below.

The big lads did it - Jimmy Hamilton, my brother Alex, Jackie Thom, Jimmy Donaldson, Davie Ritchie, Alex Cameron, and gradually it worked down to us younger boys. But then, disaster struck, as it so often did when we boys were doing something interesting. One of the jumpers hit his jaw on his knees and he bit his tongue. There was blood everywhere.

All paratroop training was postponed. In fact, the parachute brigade was disbanded, and we smaller boys never got a chance to jump. So I never did a parachute jump, and I suppose I never will. But what I've seen of parachute jumps since, I have grave doubts about the aerodynamic efficiency of that table-cloth parachute back in 1940.

Aberdeen's most famous soldier whom I'd never heard of and I suspect not many Peterhead folk had either - a Field Marshal Milne - wrote to the *Buchanie*, saying that Hitler would gamble with an invasion, no matter how many German lives it cost. Because : "German lives are only pawns in the game of the German gangster, and the stake is high." So we had to be ready for the invasion, on the alert, more than ever.

One Saturday morning there was a whirl of excitement in our streets when a number of Bren Gun carriers and army lorries came trundling down our road pulling guns on wheels. They came to a stop along the Braes between the bottom of our street and the Cable Hoosie, and the guns were unlimbered and pointed out to sea. Of course we all knew what was coming, and windows were opened - not so that those inside could hear better - but so the blast wouldn't break the glass. Then the guns started firing. I suppose they were firing blanks, but it was thrilling stuff, and the smoke blew back over the town. It was a spectacle and we enjoyed every minute of it. It took most of Saturday morning to complete the exercise, because there was more to it than just firing off shells. There were soldiers shouting commands and others running about doing things. It all looked very purposeful and very deadly. By the time they had packed up and gone back to barracks for dinner, we were looking forward to the Jerries coming so they could get their just desserts. I'm sure it was a useful exercise for the soldiers, but even more, it was a great confidence booster for the people of Peterhead.

Night after night, the air-raid sirens went, but mostly the bombers weren't coming to Peterhead or the Broch, but were using Rattray Head as a landfall point in their line of direction from Trondheim in Norway on their way to bomb other parts of Scotland or the north of England. Later in the war, when they were bombing places like Liverpool and Clydebank, they still came to Rattray Head, and of course if they didn't get to drop bombs on their targets, they would unload them on the north-east rather than take them home.

George May had wondered at the Guy Fawkes bombing in Fraserburgh how it was that humans could kill their fellow-humans without a second thought, but it was easy in war-time to forget you were dealing with human beings. We were against the Jerries, our sworn enemies, and they were against us. Yet they were human beings, just like ourselves. This was brought home to me many years later when one of our friends in the Far East was a German missionary. It was even more ironic, when later on our daughter, Ruth, was friendly with a South African boy, whose grandfather had served in the army at Dunkirk, as had our daughter's grandfather. The irony was that his was in the German army, while Ruth's was in the British...

As we approached the winter of 1940 with the threat of invasion still hanging over us, we were not thinking of the Jerries as fellow-humans. They were the enemy, pure and simple! And it was to escape their bombs that the folk of the north-east prepared to spend their winter nights in their shelters, and for the Davidson family, that meant those "mochty foons" below the Camerons' floor-boards.

Chapter 10

First encounter with my future wife

One dark night with snow lying, either late November or early December, 1940, father was late home from work. Mother was worried, what with him on his bike and the blackout and the snow, and it was snowing again, he should have been home by this time. Then we heard his bike being put behind the outside door and the welcome sound of his boots on the stairs and, and there was another sound, a thump, perhaps of firewood? But it was no firewood that father bore into the warm and gaslit kitchen. It was a sledge. A large heavy sledge, made with off-cuts of wood, with wooden runners rimmed with ribbon steel. A beautiful sledge, big enough to hold Alex and me and another passenger. I have never seen a bonnier sledge, made with loving care from salvaged wood. And it was a surprise, totally unexpected. How difficult it was to restrain from trying it out, though it had to stay indoors until daylight, and that was after school next afternoon. So it lay in the lobby and I sat on it and dreamed of swooshing down the roads of Ives Park and Ugie Park, and maybe even Windmill Brae, or as it's called nowadays, Balmoor Terrace.

Our sledge was heavy to steer. You had to sit at the back and dig your left heel into the snow to make it go to the left, or the opposite way to steer it right. But its weight meant it didn't respond easily. It took a while for the iron rims to get really slidy, but when they were coated with icy snow, the sledge could go as fast as any of the lighter ones with iron runners. We didn't name it or paint it, it was just the Sledge. Looking back, I wonder whatever happened to it... a sledge of best hardwood, made by a skilled craftsman, a sledge made to last...

From *The War Illustrated*, we'd seen armoured trains from the Russo-Finnish War. They were painted white and had big guns sticking out all over them. One of the boys suggested we make ourselves an armoured train by joining sledges together. So we tied our sledges one behind the other, about six of them. And since our Sledge was the heaviest, it went first. Which meant when the "train" was going, I was seated cross-legged right at the front, a dangerous position though that never occurred to me at the time. When we were all on board and rumbling down Ives Road, it really felt like an armoured train. Maybe even sounded like one.

Who were the personnel on that Armoured Train? I would guess that apart from Alex and me, there was Jimmy Hamilton, the Cameron boys, Alex and Simon, Davie Ritchie and his younger brother Jimmy, and maybe Andy, though he might have been too young. Then certainly there had been Jackie Thom, probably Jimmy Donaldson from across the Blinner, maybe Bertie Williams, and his younger brother, Billy. And Breezy McLean. We were a fairly active bunch of lads, inventive and forever making our own fun, because there was no television and computer games in those days, and precious little else to play with apart from some big brother's football from pre-war days, and wooden-boxes and pram wheels from the rubbish tip, and fishing lines and a length of clothes-line for "catching salmon".

Air-raid warnings were sounding most nights, but the Jerries were not visiting Peterhead. The air-raid Alerts sounded because Peterhead was on their route to Clydeside and Liverpool. I wondered how our evacuees were getting on in Glasgow, because it was getting bombed now. It was a comfort to know that the RAF were hammering German cities. Every night they were bombing the Jerries, at least the wireless said so, but that was little comfort to the thousands killed in Britain that November, and the even larger number who were seriously injured.

About Christmas time, a German we'd never heard of though he became famous later, a man called Rudolf Hess, made a speech about God making the Jerries better than every one else so they were bound to win the war. But our King said God was going to help us beat the Jerries and we all knew our King was right. So that Christmas of 1940, both the Germans and the British claimed to be the special favourites of God.*

Our armoured train was great, so we decided to try it on another street. We wanted to go up Windmill Brae, but mother and father would never allow us up there. It was too long and steep and sometimes there was traffic on it, horse-carts and things. I don't know if the other boys risked Windmill Brae, but the Davidson boys stuck to Ives Road. Though there was no problem going down the Second Streetie : Raemoss Road today. So to the Second Streetie we pulled our Armoured Train, along past Reid's Shoppie, and at the top of the road we poised to conquer new pastures, in a manner of speaking. There it was, a brand new street stretching before us, so we linked our Armoured Train, the Davidson heavy sledge leading the way, and myself perched at the front.

It was an ordinary ride. We trundled off and gathered speed and the wind whipped past us, and we shouted and cheered and felt very brave, because this was foreign territory, not our own street at all. Everything was going great, until I realised from my better view right at the front, that disaster loomed ahead.

Half-way down the road, hard against the pavement on our left, was a wee girl, wrapped up against the cold in coat and scarf and pixie, with a small sledge. She was a lonely wee figure as she looked at us in horror hurtling towards her. Our sledge was difficult to steer. Normally we just bounced off the pavement with no harm done, but this time there was a wee bairn between us and the pavement. And in the seconds I saw it, there was nothing anyone could do. We hit her, and she and her sledge went flying.

"a wee girl, wrapped up against the cold - with a small sledge"

To the foot of the road we rumbled, shocked into silence while all was silent behind us. Not even a howl from the bairn. Then dismantling the Armoured Train we fled with our sledges, pursued by guilt. We were silent over the mishap. And the Armoured Train never appeared on the streets of Peterhead again.

The end of the story? Not quite. I had been married to Jean Wilson, my girl-friend from Raemoss Road, for twenty-seven years, when one evening I happened to notice that the pinky on her right hand was out of line with her other fingers. So I asked her what had happened to it. And she told me. She told me when she was a wee girl her father had made her a sledge, just big enough to take her and one of her young brothers. She remembered being in the roadway outside her home - her brothers were getting put to bed and she was taking the opportunity to play with the sledge by herself - when this sledge-train laden with big boys came hurtling down on her and knocked her to the pavement and she was unconscious and taken to the hospital with a broken finger. And she remembered the doctor asking her if she had sent her letter up the lum to Santa, while he reset her finger. Ouch! I was squirming.

What could I say? I confessed my part in the crime, and she forgave me; forgave me for the manner of our first meeting. Our next meeting was in the Buchanness Ballroom, Boddam, but that was thirteen years later and a different story altogether...

One of the first things that happened in 1941 was that we got sandbags, two per family, and they were for dumping on an incendiary bomb if it landed on our house. The idea was that it would take two sandbags to smother the incendiary because nothing else could extinguish it, especially not water which otherwise was all we had. And the Germans had lots of incendiaries. In fact, the town of Plymouth had twenty thousand incendiaries dropped on it in one night, though I can not remember any incendiaries being dropped on Peterhead. It was mostly high-explosives we received, and they were bad enough. We saw the incendiaries at the Pictures, usually in a Ministry of Information film, and it showed you how to deal with them. The idea was that the sulphur in the bomb burned through the sacking cover and then the sand smothered it.

Our two sand-bags languished in a cupboard in the lobby, and later in the war they made a smashing north African desert in a tray for my toy soldiers of the "Desert Rats" - our Eighth Army - to beat Rommel and his Afrikakorps. But that January of 1941, we had never heard of Rommel, and the Jerries were nowhere in Africa, and it was just the Italians we were fighting there, and beating them hands-down everywhere: Tobruk, Benghazi, Ethiopia, though these were just names to feed my imagination. But every news-time, we heard of raids on English cities and

Clydeside, and hundreds of citizens, many of them children, being killed by the Nazi bombers.

Mr Yule, the minister of the East Parish church - it's called St Andrew's now - dedicated an ambulance which had been given to Peterhead by friends of the town who lived in New York. It was encouraging to know that the Americans were on our side, and even their leader, President Roosevelt, said they would make sure we had all the weapons we needed to fight Hitler.+

Meanwhile, the most common crime in Peterhead during the early days of 1941 seemed to be letting light shine from your house during black-out hours, because there was often a bunch of offenders up in court. But there was no doubt, letting light shine from the town during the darkness could attract the Jerry bombers. We had a bad example of it from the Guy Fawkes night bombing of the Broch when the bombers were attracted by a fire.

Though the most memorable bombing in the opening weeks of 1941 in the north-east took place during daylight. It was when a farm was bombed, but the *Buchanie*, obeying the censorship law, never told us where the farm was. Two bairns, Jimmy Gall and his sister, Betty, had just gone out to the tap to get pails of water when a German bomber dived on them. A bomb fell in a nearby field and Jimmy shouted to his wee sister to "flop!" but she was so excited she ran about the farm-yard. "We certainly got a big scare," said Jimmy. No wonder, because the enamel was actually blown off the pails they had been carrying. Unfortunately, a man working nearby was killed but the *Buchanie* never gave his name and there is no record of him anywhere. Perhaps he was an Italian prisoner of war, because very large numbers of Italians had been captured in North Africa, and it was not unusual for some of them to volunteer to work on farms. And of course, as a POW, he would not be recorded as a civilian casualty.

The next bombing of Peterhead - and again the town was never mentioned, though we all knew where it was - the next bombing was in March, on Friday, 7th March, to be precise. A bomber flew over the town in the morning and dropped two bombs on the Links, close to the old cemetery. I suppose they were trying to get the woollen mill, but the explosives fell in the soft earth and did little damage. What damage that did occur was to the roof of a shed in the mill where Herbie Cruickshank was working. I used to work with Herbie and he never mentioned his close encounter with the Jerries, nor about the roof falling in on him.

William Blyth who worked in the cemetery saw the Jerries coming and threw himself behind a grave-stone. He was closer to the bomb-bursts than Herbie, but he also was unhurt because granite gravestones and a strong wall can fairly block the blast of high explosive. The Muckle Kirk manse had its windows and walls spattered with clay from the links, but all in all, Peterhead got off lightly from that bombing raid.

We made jokes about the war. I must be showing my age because I still think they're funny. Here is one: Dr Taylor: "Your throat is very bad. Have you tried gargling with salt and water?"

Seaman Buchan: "Yes. I was torpedoed last week."

And another one, though this was from my Father from the trenches in the 1914-18 War:

Private McTavish has visited the Medical Officer and is trying to get sent to hospital to get him out of the front-line. So the doctor asks him: "And how are your lungs, Private McTavish?"

And Private McTavish: "I can hardly speak with my right lung," he croaks. Then he adds loudly: "But I can speak perfectly all right with my left lung."

It was gallows humour, the irrepressible human spirit that sees something funny in the direst of situations. Maybe a sense of humour was in great demand that winter, because things were not going too well with our soldiers in Greece, nor in North Africa now that Field Marshal Rommel and his German panzers had landed there to help the Italians, and raids on British towns and cities were increasing in severity. Even Japan was starting to throw its weight about in the Pacific, though not actually starting a war against us.

Nearer home, tragedy struck in Cruden Bay. The Jerries bombed the brickworks on the 2nd April, and machine-gunned the village. There were five casualties, two of whom were fatal, John Mcleod of the Royal Observer Corps, and 78-years old James Gray .

The Broch was again the target for a daylight raid, on Saturday the 5th April, and the target was Maconnachies food preserving factory. Maconnachies provided tinned food for the forces as I experienced for myself some years later in the Middle East - when we used to get Maconnachies steak and kidney pie, cold, and served up sometimes for breakfast as well as for dinner. But the factory was a target for the Jerries in 1941, and two women, Mrs Jean Booth Simpson, a forewoman, and Miss Elizabeth Sim, who had been working in an upper floor, were killed when a bomb hit the building. Mrs Jessie Dunbar and Mrs Christian Michael died from their injuries in Foresterhill Hospital next day, the Sunday, and the following Tuesday, Agnes Nicol of Gardenstown, who had also been injured in the bombing died from her injuries. There was a large number of casualties from that raid, but they survived. I heard that the German plane also machine-gunned Cairnbulg and Inverallochy before it disappeared out to sea, but I could not verify that because censorship never revealed the names of towns or villages.

NOTES

*Rudolf Hess in a Christmas Eve message to the German people: "Divine Justice has turned against England. We are carrying on the fight in the belief in the superior value of our people. For the Almighty has also created the German people; and service for this people is thus also service in the belief in the Almighty who created it."

And King George VI, in his Christmas Day message, said: "The future will be hard, but our feet are planted on the path of victory, and with the help of God we shall make our way to justice and to peace."

+President Roosevelt, on 29 December, 1940, broadcast: "We must be the arsenal of the democracies."

Chapter 11

Bombing raids

March 1941: Guess who said this: "Eternal providence does not let those be victorious who are ready to shed the blood of men merely for the attainment of their own ends"? Hard to believe, but that was Adolf Hitler in a speech on March 16. Just goes to show that even he was right some of the time, though he had prefaced that statement by saying: "England will fall." By 'England' of course, he meant Britain and her empire.

But Hitler was ready to shed the blood of men - and of women and children. In the Broch, apart from the women who were killed in the April raid on Maconnachies, there were more casualties later that month, Thursday 17 April, to be precise. Six women were killed by a bomb on Castle Street where a house was demolished and two others badly damaged, and a wee bairn, five-year old Millicent Dunbar, who was injured at the same time, died the next day in the Sick Children's Hospital, Aberdeen. Apparently one of the women had been shielding Millicent with her body, and the wee girl was taken out of the wrecked house after three hours of digging. There was a lucky escape for a lady, a Mrs Wallace, who also lived in the block. She had taken her two children out with her for some shopping so that she could finish off her spring-cleaning. She was on the way home when the bomb fell and put an end to her spring-cleaning. That was the only day-time raid on Britain that day, and it gave the lie to Hitler's self-righteous nonsense condemning those who were prepared to shed the blood of men.

The following Sunday, Aberdeen was bombed and machine-gunned, and although ten people were injured, there was only the one fatality - three-years old Alistair Watson, of Urquart Road. Come to think of it, in both these raids, no men had been killed. It was women and children who died, while Hitler had spoken about shedding "the blood of men." I'm not sure if it's the war that makes monsters out of men, or if it is the monster in men which makes the war. Probably it's a bit of both.

The month of March had been a bad month for the Allies, with German and Italian advances in the Balkans and Rommel's Afrika Korps pushing us back in North Africa. There was one British victory when the Royal Navy inflicted a heavy defeat on the Italian navy at Cape Matapan south of Greece. The story is that the British naval commander, Admiral Sir Andrew Cunningham, was going to sail with his fleet out of Alexandria to meet the Italian ships which had been spotted by a Sunderland flying boat. The problem was that he wanted it to be a surprise attack, and he knew the Japanese consul in Alexandria reported all movements of British ships to the Germans, so on the afternoon before he slipped out of Alexandria harbour, he went to the local golf club with a suitcase as if he intended spending a few days ashore. By this ruse, he succeeded in pulling wool over the eyes of the Japanese, and the attack on the Italians was a complete surprise.

April was another bad month for us. The Jerries had pretty well taken over Yugoslavia and Greece, and Rommel had pushed us right back in North Africa. Our army still held out at Tobruk but was completely surrounded by German and Italian forces. And there were heavy air-raids on Britain, especially on London. Around Peterhead, long poles sprouted, sticking up into the sky wherever there was an open grassy space. These were for piercing German gliders carrying airborne troops in the event of an invasion, and they also made life difficult for anyone on a parachute. If I remember correctly, it was about this time that prisoners of war - Germans I think, because they were wearing hats like those in the Afrika Korps - commenced work building big concrete gun-emplacements along the Gadle Braes where the pumping station now stands between Buchanhaven and Ugie Park.

These prisoners were a source of fascination to us. They were Jerries and we would not have been surprised to see them sprouting horns. But they seemed almost like human-beings, though we did not go too close to them. Can't say the same for the wee girl, Jean Wilson, I was later to marry. She watched these foreigners with fascination, and one of them eventually managed to entice her to approach close enough for him to show her a photograph from his pocket, a photograph of his little daughter back home who looked something like her. Since those days I have learned that prisoners-of-war can not be made to help the war effort of the enemy nation, but somehow these men worked on Britain's defences. After the emplacements were built, two huge guns were placed in them, their barrels pointing out towards Rattray Head. They were really big guns, with barrels like the ones at the front of a large battleship.

Once the guns were in place and the prisoners-of-war had long since been taken back to the POW camp - I think it was out beside Stuartfield though I could not be sure of that - one Saturday morning a policeman came round on a bike blowing his whistle and telling everyone to open their windows. Why? Because the big guns were going to be test-fired.

So why open the windows? Because if windows were closed, they would break with the force of the blast. So the windows were opened, the guns fired, and the noise was tremendous, but I don't remember any windows breaking.

An important gentleman in the Government, a Mr Herbert Morrison, announced that Fire-watching would no longer be voluntary. It was to be compulsory. Since Father had been Fire-watching at the harbour for some time that made no difference to our family. The compulsory Fire Watching order covered 18-60 year olds, though there were instances of 16-year-old boys doing it. There had been a bit of a dispute because Fire-Watchers were being paid in Fraserburgh but not in Peterhead. But with the new Fire-Watching Order which required 48 hours of fire-watching duty a month, payment would be made. So Mr Morrison had resolved that dispute. But that gentleman said something else which was an inspiration to us bairns. He launched the slogan: "Britain shall not burn!" Which was quite a boast considering that much of London and Coventry and Clydebank and Plymouth had gone up in flames. But it was the inspiration we Blinner boys needed. We would have our own Fire-engine. And like the Armoured Train of sledges, our Fire-engine would be a co-operative affair.

It would consist of our hurdies tied together in a train. A hurdie was

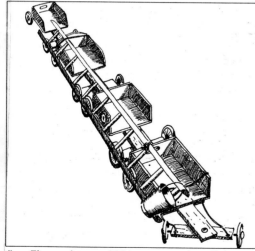

"our Fire-engine would be a co-operative affair"

basically a fish-box bolted on to a long plank with pram-wheels and axles at the front and back. The front axle was held by a large staple which allowed it to steer with play to the right or left, usually by means of a rope tied to the axle just inside where the wheels were fixed. It meant that you could sit in your fish-box and steer your vehicle. So there you have it, a train of hurdies joined together, the basic foundation of our Fire-engine.

Every self-respecting fire-engine has a ladder and a hose-pipe, but this was no problem because the Cameron boys had contacts, and in due time they produced the required accoutrements of a real fire-engine. So there we were, ready with hurdies, ladder and hose - no water, but that was a mere detail - and we were ready to tackle any fire, preferably one at the bottom of Ives Road. Of course, before you can put out a fire, you have to try out your fire-engine. And that is what we did. We piled on to it, and there were the usual five or six fire components joined together - hurdies, that is. And we pushed off from the top of Ives Road.

Our Fire-engine could go fast. Down the road we swished, and if any parents had been watching, their hearts would have been in their mouths. The wind was whistling by us and we were living out in our imagination a ready response to that slogan: "Britain shall not burn." All the way down the road, moving faster now, and of course no traffic of any kind to be seen. And at the bottom, we would turn either to the right or the left, it was all one. Except for one thing. The driver at the front - I have no idea who it was, but it wasn't my brother Alex for our hurdie was near the back - our driver could not turn the Fire-engine's steering gear. Straight on we went, heading for the pavement which ran parallel with the rocks and the sea.

Crash! We hit the pavement at speed and there was a violent loss of equilibrium. Some of us fell off on to the grassy bank, and others with admirable quick-thinking followed suit and baled out. Faster than it takes to say, the entire crew of the Fire-engine had abandoned it while it careened on, gaining speed, down the steep grassy bank, hit the low dyke at the bottom, then catapulted into space to land on the chingle and rocks beside the Mountainy - the Ive Rock. Our Fire-engine suffered serious damage. It never recovered. The ladder and the hose-pipe were restored to their rightful owner. Mr Morrison would have to do without our help, as we nursed our minor bruises. "Peterhead shall not burn!" would be the responsibility of our fathers and big brothers who were Fire-watching, and of the NFS - the National Fire Service.

It was only in recent years that I discovered the answer to something which puzzled me when I was a child. We had been friendly with a family in Boddam, though I think the friendship went back to before I was born, and possibly to when my parents had lived in Aberdeen. The family were the Pirie family, Jim and Mary Pirie, and their children, some of whom were grown up and away in the forces. And there came a time when what I remember was Mrs Pirie being tearful and upset and there was a certain amount of coming and going then I think she moved away from Boddam. I can remember very little of Mr Pirie except that he was a quiet man, and nice and friendly. After a time we seemed to lose touch with the family.

When I was researching the lists of civilian casualties from German bombing, I came across the following reference:

First Aid Post, St Peter Street, 100841

Pirie, James William (57) Royal Observer Corps, 3 Manse Terrace, Boddam, Peterhead. Injured 16/5/41 @ Observer Post, Stirling Hill, Boddam - died 17/5/41 @ 3 Manse Terrace.

There was no reference to his death in the press, nor of a bombing attack. But now I can understand why Mary Pirie went through a tearful time and why my parents were so comforting towards her. Without the brief reference copied above there might have been no other memorial to a local man who sustained fatal injuries due to enemy activity while at his post of duty. I remember him only as a quiet, decent man.

In July, the people of Peterhead and the surrounding villages enjoyed a respite from the strains of war by attending the Aikey Fair. Some two hundred horses were sold at that fair at prices ranging from £80 to £142, and for so many horses to change owners just goes to show how dependent we were on four-footed transport. All the heavy work on farms and around the town, and even the grocery-and vegetable and coal mannies who came round the streets had their vehicles pulled by horses. My wife, Jean, tells me that as a child she used to feed "Queenie", the horse that pulled the Co-op van, with grass from her front garden, much to the consternation of its driver who would be serving a customer at the back when the horse would mount the pavement to get the delicacy Jean was offering it.

Air raids were becoming more frequent now. It was common for sirens to sound during the day or the night, though not many of the bombers actually dropped their bombs on Peterhead. At night it was usually bombers coming over us on their way to somewhere else. During the day-light hours, the raids were usually on convoys of ships on the horizon. There was a raid on the Broch in July when an elderly couple, James Smith and his wife, Helen, were killed at 17 Commerce Street. Thirteen people were injured in that raid, including Mr Rae, a dairyman, who was hit a quarter mile away by a stone thrown from the explosion.

In August, Peterhead was bombed, though whether it was a deliberate raid, or a bomber jettisoning a stick of bombs rather than take them back to Norway I don't know. The pattern of the bombs landing suggested it was indiscriminate bombing. Since it was early on Sunday morning, I suspect it could have been a chance raid by someone who had not found his target elsewhere. The bombs were dropped across the town by a low-flying plane. A building was blown up and fell on top of a First Aid Post in St Peter Street - the old soup kitchen - where some forty people were working. A Voluntary Aid Detachment nurse, 59-years old Mrs Taylor, of Constitution Street, was killed at this FAP. Two men, Mr James Mitchell and Mr A. McAllister were saved from falling masonry when steel shelving came down on them and shielded them. Another man was found inside the bomb crater. Two girls, Miss Wellburn and Miss Cowe, were trapped in the debris and after they managed to get themselves free, they worked on amongst the wrecked building helping to rescue others.

By a strange coincidence, though the bombs fell well apart, the bomb that fell in Queen Street, landed on the home where James Mitchell's wife, Annie, and her seven-years old son, James, were visiting her mother. Her mother, Mrs Annie Keith, died in the explosion, but the Mitchell family, James at the First Aid Post, and his wife and son in Queen Street, survived the attack.

I think it was the bomb on Queen Street which presented me with a temptation. The following day, I was going up the L-shaped lane from Queen Street which comes out on King Street opposite what used to be the North School. There was debris from the bombed house on Queen Street lying about the lane, and down beside a telegraph pole was a book - about Robin Hood. It was lying open at a picture, and it looked a really desirable thing to possess, and I've always loved books. I picked it up, then I thought of its owner - bombed by the Jerries - then I reverently laid the book back down where it had been, still open at the picture. I wonder whatever became of it...

The third bomb was responsible for me seeing my first dead person. In North Street, Thomas Hamilton lived along with his daughter, Mrs Jean

Murray, her husband, James, and their two children. When the siren went, James decided to go out into North Street to see what he could see, and he took their two-years old son with him. He had just reached the street when his home erupted behind him in a great explosion. It had received a direct hit from a high-explosive bomb. His father-in-law Thomas, his wife, and his seven-months old daughter, Myrna, died in the blast. His wife was found lying protectively over the corpse of their infant daughter.

Our downstairs neighbours in Ives Park were related to Mr Hamilton - in fact I think he was their paternal grand-father - and his body was taken to lie in its coffin in their kitchen/living room. All we bairns round the doors were invited in to see old Mr Hamilton, a victim of Hitler and his Luftwaffe. I am not sure why we all had to see the corpse. Perhaps it was to impress on us the seriousness of war, or maybe to reinforce our hatred for the Jerries. But the lasting impression I had was to question how a living person could become such a cold, grey thing as a dead body. And perhaps at that young age there was planted in me a deep conviction that man is more than just a physical being, that there has to be something of man which survives death. I had never known Mr Hamilton in life, but I was absolutely sure there was more to him than this husk of a body lying in its coffin, this victim of our hated enemies, the Germans.

It has only occurred to me - the three bomb sites, Queen Street, the First Aid Post on St Peter Street, and the house in North Street, they lie in almost a straight line. It really was a stick of bombs.

Chapter 12

"A crime without a name..."

The first time a Jerry bomber came over Peterhead was that time when we had the girl evacuees from Glasgow staying with us, and the air-raid siren went just as the plane dropped its bomb at the Gadle Braes. But there was another time when I don't remember the siren going at all, and that was in the spring of 1941, sometime in April. I was in bed, and I thought it was early morning with the light coming in. Anyway, I was aware of the roar of a plane flying low overhead and it went off towards the harbour. Then came the loud explosion, and we thought: "The harbour's got it!" But it hadn't. What did happen was that the plane dropped a bomb, aiming for the slipway, and if it had hit its target it would have made some mess because there were boats up the slip and the concrete flooring would have magnified the blast. But the bomb fell short, into the soft soil of the rail terminus where the coal was stored for the boats. There was a blast right enough, but the shunnery soil between the railway lines smothered the explosion a bit. What did happen was that pots of paint stored at the slipway were thrown about, and the wooden walls of a herring gutting yard across the road were splashed with different colours of paint. It was a bit of a laugh in the town.

I was speaking recently with Agnes Strachan, a local councillor, about that bomb, and she remembered it clearly. Her family lived in Great Stuart Street, just across from where the bomb fell. All the windows in her house were blown in, and she and her two sisters who were sleeping in a bed-settee in the front room had a near thing. The glass of the window came in but the high back of the settee protected them and the shards fell at the bottom of the settee where their feet were protected by the bed-clothes. A close thing for three wee girls.

Speaking of that gutting yard reminds me of the gang hut we had in a disused fish-yard on Ugie Street. One of the big shutters on to the pavement was loose, so we were able to push it open and climb inside, and in that smelly yard we had our secret meetings. There was a gang of us from the Blinner, and what we did there was simply sit and talk and plan whatever boys planned in those days. It would have had something to do with fighting the Jerries if they invaded us. But the real reason we went into that yard was because we thought it was forbidden and very risky. We didn't do any vandalism - I don't think the word had been coined in those days, certainly not in Peterhead - and we always left things as we found them. The whole point about having a secret den is that no one should ever know you've been there, and no one knows when you are there. So we were very quiet. And very secret.

We did forge an alliance with the railway gang for a short time, but it only lasted a week or two, then that palled on us. The point is, the railway gang, whose fathers were connected with the railway station, used to meet in a hut just about where the DIY firm is nowadays, across from the Safeway car park. That was a rather posh place, a real hut, but there was no thrill about doing something risky or forbidden meeting in that place. And since it was an alliance that just talked, it soon fizzled out.. And in later years I used to see some of the railway boys about the town, but there was no recognition on either side. We simply had little in common.

I think it was in the autumn that brother, Willum, was told he was going to Singapore on a troop-ship along with hundreds of other soldiers to help build up the garrison there. This was at a time when the Japanese were making threatening sounds in the Pacific. He was lined up on the quay with the other soldiers ready to board the troopship when he along with a handful of others were told they were not going to Singapore but they had to report back to their units. Apparently, there are always spare people added on to the strength of a draft just in case some of the soldiers who were supposed to go didn't come back from leave - they go AWOL (absent without leave) and the additional ones had to make up the shortfall. Sufficient numbers of the draft turned up so Willum and a handful of other soldiers did not sail for Singapore. He was not pleased about this because he was bored with being on the anti-aircraft guns in Orkney and he had seen Singapore as an escape from the monotony of a home posting. But it turned out in the long run to have been a fortunate break for him because he would have been there when the Japanese invaded and captured it.

There was not much good news on the radio towards the end of summer, 1941. The Russians were being driven back by the Germans and it looked as if Hitler would beat Stalin. But there were some items of good news: one was that British, Canadian and Norwegian Commandos had attacked the island of Spitzbergen which the Jerries had taken from Norway. Our boys did a lot of damage and got away again. It looked at that time as if the Commandos, and the RAF bombing Germany, were the only ones who were winning victories against the Jerries. Other good news was that if children were tall for their age, they were to get extra

"I was tall for my age". The author is on left with his pal, Jimmy Ritchie, on his right.

clothing coupons, and I was tall for my age. Mother was very pleased with the additional coupons my extra inches gained her. Another bit of good news was at the end of August, figures of casualties of bombing raids were released which showed a real drop in casualty numbers compared with July. Even if the figures weren't real and they were made smaller just for propaganda purposes, it was still encouraging to know that casualty numbers were falling. Of course, if you were one of the casualties the smaller number was no comfort to you.

On a Friday morning at the beginning of September, the Jerries returned to Peterhead. Bombs were dropped about Rose Street and it is likely the target was the shipping in the harbour, but the bombs landed on buildings. It was a miracle no one was killed, although two men, Joseph Elston and Alfred Brown were badly injured.. But an awful lot of seagulls were killed. The tall roofs must have been covered with the birds because after the explosion their feathers were falling everywhere like snow. Mr John Hepburn the butcher had a near thing because he had been working in his back shop and when heard the plane he ran through to the front shop. "I dived under the counter when the bomb exploded. Glass and debris flew everywhere but I was unhurt," he said. And if he had remained in the back shop the chances were he would have been killed because that part of the shop was wrecked. It sounded like a joke but it was deadly serious, when he remarked: "I doot I'll need to shut my shop the day." And the reply was: "Ye'll hae some difficulty daein that.. ye've nae doors or windows left." A sense of humour came in handy at times.

Later that month, 29th September, James Street in Peterhead was bombed. The local press announced simply that a north-east town had been bombed and a large number of civilians who were sheltering in the ground floor of a tenement were killed when the tenement received a direct hit. In some instances, whole families were wiped out. The press went on to say:

"We are not permitted to give the names of all who were killed nor to indicate their number - instead we offer our silent sympathy in the face of what Mr Churchill has described as 'a crime without a name.'"

Here are the names of those who died, with their ages:

Isabella Whyte Barron (69)
William Barron (69)
Edith Cormack Cameron (6)
James Lees Cameron (2)
Jessie Scott Cameron (40)
Lorna Cameron (12 months)
Henry Charles Chalmers (7)
Marjory Angus Chalmers (4)
Sheila Chalmers (11)
Jessie Cormack (64)
Agnes Clark Duncan (20)
Isabella Nora Hutcheson Duncan (38)
John McQueen Duncan (19)
Margaret Isabella Duncan (17)
Andrewina Bruce Geddes Lacey (5)
Margaret Buchan Lacey (11)
May Buchan Lacey (3)
Sarah Bruce Lacey (33)
Jane Anne Brown Porter Lawson (6)
Douglas McKay (3)
Gladys Wilson McKay (7)
Jean McKay (36)
Alexander Mackie (47)
Isabella Jane Mackie (48)
Williamina Elizabeth Milne (50)
Henry Charles Shepherd (63)
Margaret Jane Craig Shepherd (60)
Williamina Strachan (45)

Helenora Watson (46)

These are the casualties who died at Nos. 5, 9 and 11 James Street, Peterhead on the evening of Thursday, 29 September, 1941.

William Watson (50) was injured at 9 James Street, and died the following day in the Royal Infirmary, Aberdeen.

That makes a total of 30 victims of the bomb - though some say it was not a bomb but a parachute mine aimed at the harbour - and of that total, twelve of them were under 12 years of age.

Stories were told of the bombing, of how an elderly man refused to get out of bed when the siren went, and of how he was spared when the part of the building where his family had gone to shelter was hit and they were all killed while his house was unscathed. Or of the girl working in the **Regal Cinema**, when the Alert went and the film was shut off and the lights went up, and she had the choice with all the staff and audience of remaining in the cinema or going home, and how she chose to remain. And by so choosing, her life was spared, but she lost all her family except for her father who had gone back from leave only days before to his unit in the army.

It was a black day for Peterhead. The town was shocked into mourning, especially with so many small children being killed. And there was n o

James Street, Peterhead. 29 September 1941

mortuary in the town large enough to hold all the bodies. The police station or the cottage or fever hospitals could not cope. So an emergency mortuary was pressed into service. This was a disused herring-gutting yard at the top of Ugie Street, next door to the Faith Mission Hall, and only a yard or two up from the one which housed our gang hut.

We bairns, as ghoulish as only bairns can be, were driven by curiosity to explore the new "mortuary". Up Wilson Road we crept, and peered through cracks in the fencing into where herring used to be gutted and packed in barrels of salt. What had been benches were pressed into service and were now in lines and laden with burdens covered with white sheets. These had to be the James Street bombing victims. We were shocked into goggle-eyed silence. Then someone spotted us and chased us off. By strange coincidence, that yard and impromptu mortuary became a part of an undertaker's premises in later years. It seemed that Tom Hamilton, the first air-raid victim we had seen, had not put us off seeing more of the victims of the Jerry bombers. But it probably made us hate these Jerries even more if that were possible.

At the end of September, two items were reported which should have been good news for us and been an indication of the way the war was going, though it was easy to miss their significance at the time. The first was that the snowfall of the Russian winter had begun in the Ukraine. And the second, that the number of deaths of British civilians from German air-raids in September was again down. But that second item would have been lost on the people of the north-east with the bombing casualties of the Broch and Peterhead still fresh in our minds.

Chapter 13

Damage from friendly fire

The winter of 1941/42 approached, with night-time air-raid sirens disturbing our sleep but no bombs being dropped on Peterhead or the Broch as far as I can remember. There were certainly no casualties. In fact, the James Street bombing marked the end of deaths in Peterhead from enemy bombing. Sirens kept on sounding, but the most of the enemy action was elsewhere - either out at sea with convoys being attacked, or bombers flying high overhead making for targets in the south and west. But there were still deaths among the civilian population of Peterhead.

I think it happened on the last Sunday in November. And it involved the family we had swapped houses with back in 1939 - the Reekie family. They had exchanged their house in Ives Park with our allocated house in Hope Street. And it seems that one of the Reekie boys, James, aged 13, and his pal, John Paul, 11 years, had gone Ower the Watter, perhaps to see if anything had been washed up on the beach. But since the time of the apples and sardines and tallow flotsam, large sections of the bents along by the beach had been sown with mines and surrounded by barbed wire. Apparently the two boys had gone into an area marked off by barbed wire, one near the Jinnies Burn, and accidentally stepped on a mine. There was an explosion and they were injured. The story goes that a serviceman who had been involved in laying the mines was ill in the Cottage Hospital, and he volunteered to go into the mined area to rescue the boys because he knew where the mines had been laid. And a local shepherd, Donald Forsyth, went to help. But the shifting of the sand had moved the mines and the serviceman - I thought he was a soldier but he may have been an airman - he, too, stood on a mine, and this time, both boys and serviceman were killed, and Mr Forsyth was seriously injured.

In Ives Park, we heard the distant explosion, and we could see the smear of smoke in the distance. I don't know if it was the first or second explosion we heard, but we never paid much attention to bangs from Ower the Watter because it was not unusual for a mine to explode, perhaps when a rabbit or a deer had stood on one. But when the news of the deaths spread, it was a dampener on the town and made Ower the Watter more "out of bounds" than ever.

We were getting a mixture of good and bad news from the wireless in the closing months of 1941. In Russia, the Jerries were getting bogged down in rain and mud, and the narrow tracked tanks of Wehrmacht couldn't cope with the boggy surfaces, while the broad-tracked Russian tanks skated over the top. Then Old Man Winter hit Russia with a vengeance. Temperatures were falling to 30degrees centrigrade below freezing and Jerry tanks would not start and their guns would not fire with the cold. So the Russian army was counter-attacking and pushing back the German advance which at one stage had been 26 miles from Moscow's Red Square, at the end of a Moscow city bus-route. A Russian general said the Germans had made the great mistake of issuing their soldiers with boots which fitted them. Russian soldiers had boots far too large, with room for straw and wool to keep their feet warm. The Russians were comfortable, while thousands of Germans were crippled with frost-bite.

Two German pirate ships - armed ships which pretended to be merchant ships of neutral nations - were captured, one by the Americans and one by the Royal Navy's *HMS Devonshire*. As 1941 drew to a close, we had a feeling the war was turning in our favour. Until that summer, we were still expecting a German invasion, but as the summer passed and Hitler had his hands full in Russia, the invasion became less likely. As far as Jerries were concerned, Churchill spelled it out clearly and we all knew he was right, when he said: "In Hitler's launching of the Nazi campaign on Russia - he has made one of the outstanding blunders of history..." Jerry bombers kept coming over but we had a renewed confidence we were going to win the war.

Then the Japanese made a bigger mistake. They attacked Pearl Harbour on December 7th. They were very pleased with themselves because they had destroyed most of the American Pacific fleet in their surprise attack on the US naval base at Pearl Harbour. The Japs thought they had as good as won the war, a war started before it was even declared. But the Japs' action would cost them dearly as Hitler's attack on Russia would cost Germany.

It was all bad news from the Pacific and South East Asia. The Japanese advanced everywhere and captured whatever they attacked. Only days into war against the Japanese, the Royal Navy battleships *Prince of Wales* and *Repulse* were sunk by Jap bombers. And on Christmas Day, 1941, the British garrison on Hong Kong surrendered to the invading Japanese army.

Things were slightly better against the Germans although the British aircraft-carrier, *Ark Royal*, was bombed and sunk in the Mediterranean. British Commandos made successful raids on islands off Norway, attacking German installations, and the British garrison of Tobruk in north Afrika was relieved by our forces, and in Eritrea the remaining Italian soldiers surrendered to Allied troops, and the Italian Colony of East Africa ceased to exist. But there was no glimmer of hope in the war against Japan apart from one slight victory when British soldiers stopped the all-conquering Japanese at Bokpyin and made them retreat back into Thailand; a small reverse for the all-conquering Nips. The nine o'clock news was gloomy listening for us as 1941 drew to a close.

Hitler made a prophetic speech on Hogmanay Day, 1941, though he never guessed the full significance of what he was saying. "He who fights for the life of a nation, for her daily bread and her future, will win,(meaning himself) but he who, in this war, with his Jewish hate seeks to destroy whole nations will fail." (referring to Churchill, and now Roosevelt, both supposed to have a hatred against Germany given them by the Jews) . But his speech could also be interpreted to mean the nation who hated the Jews, and that according to Hitler was Germany. Whatever was implied by that amazing speech came back on him in full measure.

On the Home Front, bad news was common-place. It was an everyday but dreaded sight, the telegram boy coming into your street and knocking on a door with a yellow envelope in his hand. That was how the War Department sent you bad news - "We regret to inform you that your husband - your son —— has been reported killed in action...missing in action ..." For those of us who lived through those days, it was many years after the war before the sight of a telegram boy with his yellow envelope did not stir a sense of dread. Even bairns felt the dread of the telegram boy on his red bike coming into the street...they seldom brought good news. Every week there was word in the *Buchanie* of local lads missing or killed in action. Sometimes their photographs were published but I seldom knew them. But photographs were also being published of our servicemen as Prisoners of War in German camps - Stalags they were called. They were usually smiling, and they always looked smart as if ready for parade.

That winter I went to a birthday party, the first birthday party of a neighbour's baby boy. I did not really like parties, birthday or otherwise, and even now I would keep clear of social occasions if possible. Perhaps my feelings about parties date back to an experience I had at a birthday party back in 1938. There was fun and games, and one of the games involved going out of the room, and when it was your turn, you had come in and lift a fork with your mouth, and if you managed to do so, you were rewarded with your choice from a large bowl of fruit. So I was pretty confident I could lift a fork by its handle with my mouth, and I did so. Only the underside of the handle was smeared with mustard. Ugh! What a taste. But I could choose my piece of fruit, which I did. Only, it was wax fruit. Double disappointment. I can't remember if I was given a substitute piece of real fruit. That never registered with me - I can only remember the mustard and the artificial fruit. Be careful how you organise a children's party - you could be creating a lifetime complex.

So I went to the neighbour's party with little enthusiasm. There was no mustard or wax fruit, and whatever there was to eat in those days of wartime shortages was genuine. But we all had to sing or do something to entertain the party. And there was only one song I knew, so I buried my head in my arms, and sang it through:

"Roll out the Barrel, roll out the barrel of fun,
Roll out the Barrel, we've got the blues on the run,
Zing Boom Ta-Rarrel, we've got a song of good cheer,
Now's the time to roll the Barrel, when the gang's all here."

My performance was anything but a "Barrel of Fun" but I still remember it with quiet pride. My sense of duty had overcome my painful shyness. There were probably more words, but that is all I can remember. Not long after that I learned another song : "My Bonnie lies over the Ocean..." but I'll spare you that.

Jerry planes were still coming over and it could have been this winter that a low-flying plane resulted in damage to Peterhead in a daylight raid, though I can't remember it actually dropping any bomb or firing its machine-guns. It flew low over the coast and the machine-guns at the JIC opened up. The guns were aimed low to get the intruder, but no obvious hits were scored. The damage, however, did not show up until the next rainy day. A council house near the JIC began leaking water through the roof, and when the cause of the leak was investigated, it was discovered that machine-gun bullets from the JIC gun had broken tiles and some rounds had lodged in the roof. A kind of self-inflicted injury. Then there was another occasion later in the war when a ship in the south harbour opened fire on a low-flying Jerry and in swinging the gun to follow the plane, the sailors shot the top of their own mast off. That was the story in the town but I did not see the damage myself, though there are those who swear it actually happened.

I think it was about 1941 that "ch-harging" died out. And what was "ch-harging"? It was when the boys of one street or district fought with the boys from another district. I had been born in the Longate and I would have been a "Langeter" if I had stayed there. Then we moved in later years to Gladstone Road, and would have been a "Roanheider", but

"a ship in the south harbour opened fire on a low-flying Jerry-"

in flitting to Ives Park in 1939, I became a "Ugie Parker" - because Ives Park and Ugie Park were lumped together. And among our enemies we counted the "Hope Streeters", the "Battery Parkers" and the "Queenie Arabs". The thing about the "Queenie Arabs" was that with so many of them moving away from the Queenie to other parts of the town, they became fewer and fewer, so that I can not remember ever "Ch-harging" them.

My memories of ch-harging are a bit lurid, though I suspect seldom was any real damage inflicted on boys by their opponents. With some exceptions. One wintry evening of 1938/39, in a conflict with the "Battery Parkers", my brother and I were making our way back to Gladstone Road along the railway line from the coastguard station. A high fence of railway sleepers stood on end separated the road from the railway track, and Alex and I were just about to squeeze through a gap in the fence at the foot of Gladstone Road, when we were pounced on by a Battery Parker. He seemed immense to us. He towered over Alex who was only ten - he could have been left school for all we knew - and he was going to inflict punishment on Alex - I was too wee to bother with. Which was a mistake on his part. Because I had picked up on my travels a piece of iron railing, about a foot long. So when the big boy started on Alex, I came up behind him and swung my piece of metal all the way up and clouted him on the side of the head. He howled, and we fled. I threw away my weapon, and with it my guilt. Though there have been times since then I've had twinges of conscience. But I was only six ...and he was at least twice my age.

Usually there wasn't much damage done in these conflicts. One time, when our streetie were fighting the Roanheiders, as we were running up Ugie Street pursued by a larger mob, one of our number - one of our bigger boys but he's no longer with us so he shall remain nameless - tripped and fell his length. He was pounced on by the Roanheiders who began laying into him with sticks, so we halted our flight and charged back to rescue him. After his ordeal he was hardly marked, so you'll see what I mean by saying there was not much blood and gore in those encounters. Apart from my final encounter ...

We had been down the braes and suddenly stones began falling round us. It could have been Battery Parkers though I wouldn't swear to it. I couldn't throw up the brae, but the bigger boys managed it. So I was wielding a piece of iron off a barrel using it like a sword to chop up thick tungles (seaweed) into missiles for others to throw. I was safe down behind a big rock, but I wanted to see what was happening, so I popped my head up to get a good look. And that was my undoing! A stone from above hit me smack on the forehead and knocked me backwards. I howled, blood poured, and our attackers ran away. Perhaps my victim of 1938 had his revenge.

I can not recall any more ch-harging after that brief encounter. Perhaps it was the knowledge that the Jerries were trying to kill us did it. Maybe the existence of a bigger enemy than the "Queenie Arabs" or the "Battery Parkers" helped us focus our attention elsewhere - on Hitler and his Nazis. And of course we had the almost nightly reminder that they were "ch-harging" us in earnest. I believe it was that winter that the reminder came home very forcibly to the Davidson family.

My sister, Jess, and another girl, were on their way home from "the picters" in the dark, and the siren went. They were near the top of Queen Street when a Jerry plane came swooping low from the Chapel Street end, firing its machine-guns. Jess and her pal ran to one of the doors on Queen Street - all the iron palings and gates had been taken away for the War Effort - and banged on the door to get let in but it was locked. Then an ARP Warden appeared from nowhere and threw them both to the ground and covered them with himself. The Jerry flew on towards Windmill Brae and Jess and the other girl continued home. That Warden could have been risking his life to save them, and they did not even know his name - an unsung hero. War is bad, but it does have the potential to bring out noble courage from otherwise ordinary folk. Yet in us all, both the bairns of by-gone days and the bairns of today, there is the desire for violence as seen in our ch-harging. Perhaps War is simply adult ch-harging, no matter how we seek to explain it away.

Chapter 14

A bad beginning to 1942

January, 1942, was a stormy month. It was a month of snow and rain and gales of wind, some of the worst weather of the century. At one stage, all roads out of the Broch were snow-bound for days on end and the railway line to Aberdeen was blocked for almost three weeks. For a few days in the middle of January, Peterhead had no electricity because of the bad weather, and the cinemas were closed and the *Buchanie* did not appear one week. Instead, it put out a one page sheet which was free - the front page. The *Buchanie* described it as an historical event - the one page sheet, not it being free - and people were encouraged to hold on to it as a keep-sake for the future. I suppose we should have been grateful for our one-page newspaper, because that was more than the *Fraserburgh Herald* managed after the Guy Fawkes night bombing of the Broch in 1940. That bombing disaster put the *Herald* out of action for a week with no free sheet.

Electricity supplies being cut off to Peterhead did not affect the home life in Ives Park and Ugie Park because we did not use electricity, any-way. Our lighting was by gas. The gas mantle was a welcome sight when it flared into life and gave off its soft yellow illumination. And our heat-ing was by open fire - coal, firewood and shunners (coke) - which heat-ed a back boiler and gave us hot water. On a cold winter's night with the shunners banked up at a steep angle and glowing red, the water in the boiler would bubble and you could hear it through the wall. Then you would have to run off some hot water and the scullery or bathroom would fill with steam, but it was essential to save the boiler from burst-ing, or so we were told. So though the town had no electricity for a few days, it was those places powered by electricity that were affected. The North School, for example, used no electricity. The school's gas mantles were lit at noon-time to dispel the darkness of the wintry day, and the Jannie stoked the school boilers to keep the radiators hot. So although the town was without the picters - the **Playhouse** and the **Regal** were closed - and the *Buchanie* could not be published and I'm sure other places were also shut down - we bairns still had to struggle through the snow to school, scunnered by the injustice of it all.

Towards the end of January, a terrific gale struck Peterhead, driving a blizzard of snow before it. It lasted for days but the worst days were from Friday 23rd to the beginning of the following week. At times the winds reached 105 miles per hour, and with the blizzard, it was the worst weather we had seen in Peterhead for a long time, certainly the worst in my short life. It was so bad it washed away 100 feet of the breakwater. And during that tremendous storm, three cargo vessels took shelter in the Bay. Which, by the way, raises an interesting issue. Most harbours on the east coast of Scotland are closed to incoming traffic if the weather is bad enough, but I've heard it said that Peterhead Bay is never closed by bad weather. It truly is an all-weather port, and during what must have been some of the worst weather in living memory, that January of 1942, three large vessels actually made it into Peterhead's Harbour of Refuge, which is the proper name for our Bay. And two of the ships, the *S.S. Runswick* of Whitby, and the *S.S. Saltwick*, also of Whitby, which was possibly its sister ship, had actually been damaged in a collision at sea so they were in a bad way.

All three ships, the *Runswick*, the. *Saltwick*, and the *S.S. Fidra* of Glasgow, all managed into the Bay. Unfortunately, the seas inside the Bay were wild, especially with part of the breakwater washed away, and all three ships began to drag their anchors and threaten to sink. Peterhead lifeboat went out on three occasions and managed to save 106 lives. Two seamen were drowned. They had tried to make it to shore with four other seamen on a raft and when the raft neared the shore it capsized and the men were thrown into the sea. Navy men and local Peterhead men who were on the beach went into the surf and dragged the six men ashore, but only four of them were alive.

That Sunday afternoon, my father who had been out all day returned soaked to the skin and mother did not want him to go back to whatever he had been doing. It was a case of a hot bath and a dry shift of clothes but off he went back to the Bay, despite what mother said. I heard one of my uncles had been among the local men helping drag seamen out of the surf. Father never spoke of what he had been up to that Sunday, though after a time there was a printed letter in a frame on the wall of the back bedroom, but over the years it was never mentioned.

I heard a rumour many years later, however, that he had gone out on the lifeboat on one of its trips - as a volunteer - and helped save men off a ship. If that was the case, he never mentioned it to me, though older relatives do remember something. Unfortunately, it's a memory about father I can not verify though I well believe he was the kind of man to do it, because I think he was always sorry he could not go to war the fight the Jerries because of his age and health. He had gone as an under-age soldier in the First War and been wounded twice by the time he was eighteen, so he had no love for what he called the Boche, though that name was out-of-date for the Second World War. Anyway, Peterhead was battered by that ferocious storm, part of the breakwater was breached, and the men of the lifeboat service performed super-human deeds of valour. One of them, Coxswain John McLean received the lifeboat service V.C., the gold medal for gallantry, for what he did that weekend. And other crewmen received silver or bronze medals.

"the men of the lifeboat service performed super-human deeds of valour-"

It had been almost a whole month of blizzards, not the kind of weather to be out playing. But it did not stop the Luftwaffe bombing the north-east. Rosehearty was badly hit on the last Thursday in January, twelve people were killed and many more injured. A whole family, the Noble family, apart from the husband who was away at the time, were killed - the mother, Betsy Noble, and her three children, William (10), Florence (8) and George, aged three, died in the raid, along with an eleven-years old evacuee from Glasgow, Mary Leitch. Among the twelve deaths of that bombing, six were under fourteen years of age.

The terrible weather we had in the north-east was nothing compared to the wintry weather in Russia where it was helping the defenders against the Jerries. The only good news during January was coming from our Allies in Russia and we were cheered to hear that Hitler's armies were being driven back or taken prisoner or wiped out. Apart from the Russian war-front, everywhere else was bad news.

In North Africa, our soldiers were being driven back after having made advances against the Germans, and in the Far East, the Japanese were winning everywhere. The month finished with Singapore isolated and all our troops holed up there waiting to fight off a Japanese invasion. The Davidsons were more relieved than ever that Willum had been turned back at the quayside when his mates went off on their troop-ship to garrison Singapore. Gun-busking on Orkney was infinitely more desirable than facing what our boys were facing in Singapore, though before 1942 was out, we'd have more reason for worrying about Willum, though that was months away.

Funny thing is, though the war was going against us nearly everywhere, there was a big meeting in London of countries who were fighting the Germans and Italians and the Japanese, to decide what to do with Hitler and Mussolini and their pals after we won. They decided to try the leaders of the enemy countries, along with their henchmen, as criminals. So although things were going badly almost everywhere, we were still full of confidence we'd win the war.

Towards the end of January our parents were told it was their duty to go to an exhibition in the Rescue Hall to learn what to do if there was a poison-gas attack. I suppose somebody from our family went, perhaps as a distraction from the bad news we were getting on the nine o'clock news each evening. I would have thought the combination of black-outs and continuing blizzards would have kept the attendance down but no, apparently there was a good turn-out. It seemed that learning about poison-gas was even more popular than the picters. One of the events of this time was when we had to hand in our gas-masks for an additional part to be added to it. It meant that the sticky-out bit you breathed through was lengthened with a bit joined on with green insulating tape. What was it for? We were told it was to protect us against a special kind of poison gas both the Jerries and we had. Many years later doing National Service in the Royal Air Force and getting lectures on gas and such-like, we were told about that addition to the civilian gas-masks of the war-time. Apparently, the Jerries had developed a special poison gas that killed you if a drop of it came on to your bare skin and we had no answer to it. So the British claimed to have developed our own kind of poison gas, every bit as deadly as the German gas. And the additional bit on the civilian gas-masks was just a piece of propaganda of no use whatsoever. But during the war, it looked very effective and showed the Jerries we could react tit-for-tat if they used their poison gas on us. So there! It was all bluff.

The war-time introduced a number of unusual "crimes" never imagined in peace-time. We knew that letting light show after dark, no matter from what source, was a crime that could have you up before the sheriff. And also "careless talk", which meant speaking about anything which could be construed as a war secret - as for example - if Peterhead or Broch was bombed last night, or where the latest mine exploded on the coast - all secrets the Jerry should never hear about. Don't let the police or the telephone operators or anyone in authority hear you giving away such secrets.

But there was an unusual crime that could get you up in court, though it wasn't likely to bother the folk of Ives Park and Ugie Park - and that was to leave a motor vehicle parked anywhere without "immobilising" it. I can't remember anyone in Ives Park or Ugie Park in those days owning a car. We did well to have a bike in the family, never mind a car.

But for those in charge of motor vehicles, it was a duty to remove the rotor arm. Even leaving your car with doors locked and the ignition key in your pocket was not good enough. If you left the rotor arm in the engine, that was a crime. There was actually a court case in Peterhead of a Mintlaw man accused of leaving the rotor arm in his car when he parked it in Broad Street. But he got off because the police never looked under the bonnet to verify it when he admitted to them that he had not taken out the rotor arm. In court he said he had taken out the rotor arm and had it in his pocket all the time. If the rotor arm was in his pocket, he had immobilised his car. And the police never bothered to check for themselves. So he got off.

About this time Hitler had one of his mad rants against the Jews claiming they would all be destroyed: "This war will be fought in the true Biblical manner - an eye for an eye and a tooth for a tooth," he claimed. But it was he who had started it all and the Jews were not fighting him, it was the Allied Powers who were fighting him. At that time, his fight against the Jews consisted of marching off hundreds of thousands of men, women and children to death camps and their gas-chambers, though the full horrors of that would not be known until after the war. Hitler, without comprehending the full significance of what he was saying, occasionally said things that would come down on him and the German people a thousand-fold.

It was in February we were told that Allied production of planes and tanks was outstripping the war industry output of Germany and Italy, and that Japanese production of these weapons was not significant. So although things were going badly on nearly every front, the Allied home fronts, especially in America, were getting really geared up to beat our enemies. America would soon be producing as many planes as the combined outputs of the Jerries and the Japs, and the Italians too. As far as Mussolini and the Italians were concerned, even in the darkest days of the War we found it difficult to take them seriously as an enemy. In fact there used to be jokes about Italian soldiers being better at running away than fighting. I don't think it was true - in fact, they could be as brave as anyone - but the Movietone News pictures of the thousands of Italians taken prisoner in Africa certainly did nothing to dispel that belief. And it was good propaganda for the Home Front.

The air-raid sirens still sounded of an evening but the bombers were leaving us at peace for a while and sometimes we did not get out of bed to go the shelter even when the siren went. We were no longer looking for an invasion fleet on the horizon and after the snow melted and the ground dried a bit, we looked longingly at the nearby trenches and gun emplacements as possible sites for future play. But their coils of barbed wire put them out of bounds at present, and there was always just the chance they may be needed to fight the Jerries if there should be an invasion after all.

But the only Jerries we saw were prisoners-of-war. In fact, an important man in the Royal Navy had said that we could judge how well we were doing against the U-boats by counting "the fair-haired young men" being marched away under armed guard from our harbours where they had been landed. I don't remember any at Peterhead harbour, though there was that story of them being marched up George Street, Aberdeen.

The bad news of February was the fall of Singapore to the Japanese. That was headlines and everyone was talking about it. Singapore was the "Gibralter of the East", but it had been captured fairly easily because most of its defences were for repelling an invasion from the sea, and the Japs came overland. Singapore's biggest guns were destroyed without firing a shot in anger. Even the Hurricane fighters sent to defend Singapore had been transferred from the North African campaign and had been fitted to fly in a sandy atmosphere which slowed them down in the Far East. Now there was gloom and despondency about how the war was going. Thousands of our men - British, Australian and Indian - were taken prisoner at Singapore, where many of them were locked up at Changi prison, which I was to visit with my wife and children many years later. The early part of 1942 was not a happy time.

Many a Saturday afternoon after the Picters, I went into Mabins the Newsagent to buy a Ministry of Information booklet - usually costing a few pence - and read about the war in North Africa. I learned to love those names and they still ring in my memory - Mersa Matruh - Derna - Sollum - Benghazi - and best of all, Tobruk. There were always maps in those books showing the advances and retreats in the various campaigns - curving arrows showing how the armies were moving. The arrows were usually curved - perhaps artistic licence - and I could spend long minutes at a time poring over one of those maps and work out accurately who did what where and on what date. I can't remember any of it now, apart from those lovely names. And the occasional book on the

Russian front had names like Stalingrad and the Don and Kharkov. Fascinating! Conjuring up intriguing images in a child's imagination.

Chapter 15

"Very Restricted Area"

One of my prized possessions was a piece of shrapnel. At school we compared our finds, bits of bombs or shells, either found in or about Peterhead, or our big brothers or fathers had taken home from the war. My shrapnel was big enough to fill my hand and resembled the map of Australia. It had sharp edges and my brother, Willum, assured me it had been red hot when it landed and it would have cut through you like a hot knife through butter. Other boys had chunky bits of jagged metal, others had rifle bullets, and even machine-gun bullets from Jerry planes. They were big and heavy and ugly and I never liked them. One or two boys were really daring, because they had found real live rounds, the bullets in their cartridge cases with the gun-powder or cordite still in them. I remember one boy down the braes trying to make one of these rounds explode by banging it with a stone, so I made myself scarce because I didn't want to be there when it went off. But it didn't explode and maybe it wasn't a live round at all but a pretend one for the Home Guard.

Headmaster Mr Mair came round our classes to lecture us about the danger of picking up things that were lying around. The Jerries were using a funny looking bomb like a tin of beans with a straight bit sticking out and it had propellers on the end like a bairn's windmill. If we found any such suspicious object, we were not to touch it but tell a Bobby or our parents, but not touch it. Definite! These were not really bombs but booby-traps to kill civilians, in particular bairns, and they were made to look attractive to us. I never saw one in real life, but pictures of them were up on the wall of the school, and I suppose in police stations and wherever lots of people gathered. Films about them were shown at the **Playhouse** and the **Regal**, and I think we would all have recognised a booby-trap bomb if we ever found one. I suspect, however, our curiosity would have got the better of us and we'd have lifted it up for a better look. But I don't think it ever happened in our part of Scotland.

It was about this time the Davidson family was hit by dysentery. Where it came from, how we contracted it, I have no idea. The doctor's surgery was full of people with dysentery. Peterhead was under siege from it. When it hit our house, I was sent downstairs to the Hamilton's to sleep because I was not affected and it was thought if I were out of the house as much as possible, I would escape it. No such luck! It hit me just before breakfast one morning, and I joined the household of sick Davidsons. Doctor Taylor visited us and we were given a great big tin of glucose to drink with water. I couldn't understand why we had to drink glucose, but now I suppose it was to counteract dehydration. Then unexpectedly, Willum came home on leave.

What should have been a relief from war duty for him became a never-ending round of caring for his sick family. I think we were all in bed really poorly, and the toilet was in continuous use. With all the dysentery around the doctors must have been rushed off their feet. Willum certainly was, but I remember he did a tremendous job, and after a day of two of his ministrations, mother was on her feet, so was father, then the rest of us. We were wobbly on our legs, but over the worst. Peterhead gradually recovered from its dysentery, and I don't remember anyone dying from it.

Somewhere about this time I had my big secret. I used to love playing down the Braes, and at the foot of our road was a rubbish tip and we bairns plowtered about in it. Occasionally you saw rats among the garbage. And that is what I blame for my condition, which I tried to keep a secret. It started with itchy legs. So I scratched them. And they bled, they became inflamed, then developed into a rash of yellowy blisters in both legs which I kept secret. Don't ask why I had to keep it secret. But I somehow thought I had developed this as a punishment for playing on the rubbish tip in direct disobedience to mother's commands. And as long as no-one found out, I would be safe. For a week or so, I managed to keep my blistery scabby legs a secret. And I made sure no one saw me when I was having my Sunday evening bath. But it couldn't last.

"Jess, go and see if Jim is washing himself richt," said mother, and my sister came into the bathroom to check on my hygiene. She let out a scream, and it brought mother in to see what was wrong. And she was upset, too. My secret was out - the condition of my scabby legs was public property. But I did not get punished! I did not get shouted at! Instead, I was the poor bairn who was suffering, and look at his poor legs and the mess they're in. In fact, I was comforted! If I'd known this would be the grown-ups' reaction, I would have revealed my scabby legs earlier. But Doctor Gavin Taylor had the cure. The treatment was prescribed, and mother went shopping for the requisite medicine. Lysol! A big bottle of stuff resembling thin tar. And it was added to hot water in a bucket and I had to soak my legs in it for a while each evening, then my legs were bandaged.

After a week or two, the scabs fell off, and bonnie pink skin was growing where there had been suppuration. It was so good to have an easing of the itch and pain when the Lysol solution took effect, and it was good not to have that terrible scabby secret hanging over my head. Everyone was kind to me. Maybe a wee telling off, but nothing much, and just the comfort of being back in the caring bosom of the family. Bairns get so many daft ideas about guilt and secrets and getting into trouble for things not their fault. Though I have to confess that sometimes while my scabby legs were still a secret, that I would waken with the itch in the early hours and scratch them and break the heads off the beilings. And that was something I did not own up to when I was found out. I believe the proper name for what I had is scabies, or impetigo, and I know I had a bad dose of it.! But I recovered, and no more down the Braes to the rubbish tip. Which simply meant that whenever I did visit the rubbish tip in future my conscience pricked me something awful.

I wasn't much into music. I still had only the two songs: "Roll out the Barrel" and " My Bonnie lies over the Ocean". So it was quite an experience to go to the **Playhouse** and see a film called "Dangerous Moonlight", all about Poland and the war and this man playing the piano and a tune: "The Warsaw Concerto". Bairns were going about for days afterwards whistling "The Warsaw Concerto", even trying to sing it, which was quite a feat because there were no words to it, or none as I remember.

We were so impressionable. All it took was a particularly exciting film on at the picters, and we would going about for days, re-enacting it - "Mark of Zorro", (we all became the greatest swordsman in France), or "Tiger Squadron" (we were American fighter planes tearing around with arms outstretched), or "Frankenstein" - and the subsequent "Frankenstein" add-ons - and we were all clumping around, stiff-backed with arms outstretched like the monster. In one family, which shall be nameless - the girls were regularly sent into hysterics and terrified screaming by their brother pretending to be Frankenstein's monster. Strangely enough, I did meet Mr Frankenstein many years later, but he was a cultural attache at the US consulate in Hong Kong, and yes, when he told me his name, he added with a smile: "It really is Frankenstein." He was a nice enough young man.

In March, our street was plunged into gloom because a sailor, Jimmy Stewart, had been posted missing when his ship was sunk by the Japanese, and it was thought he drowned. He was only eighteen, though that was a grown-up man to me. The evening the word came, his father went and played the bag-pipes along the top of the braes, walking to and fro on the grassy bit over-looking the rocks. I think he played what is called a Lament, and maybe he was playing to express his broken heart, or maybe he was playing to his son who was somewhere way out there in a distant sea. But whatever, there wasn't a dry eye in the street or wherever the sound of that bag-pipe music reached. I can still feel sad when I remember that evening, though word eventually did come that Jimmy had been rescued from the sea and was a prisoner of the Japs, and after the War I used to see him going about. But on a bonnie spring evening in 1942, we were once again confronted with the horror of war because someone from our street had become a victim.

I heard at the time that Jimmy Stewart had been a sailor on the battle-ship *Prince of Wales*, or maybe it was the battle-cruiser *Repulse*, but they were both sunk by Japanese bombers near a place called Malaya. That was especially sad for the *Prince of Wales* because it was a new battle-ship and had fought with the German battleship **Bismarck** at the time the *HMS Hood* was sunk and not long before the **Bismarck** was also sunk. We bairns knew these names. We didn't know the things bairns know nowadays, such as footballers or pop-groups - we hadn't heard of any apart from the Ink-spots and the Andrew Sisters - but we did know our battle-ships. But then, that's the way with bairns - what interests them, they remember.

We were all cheered up when we heard that the Americans had bombed Tokyo. We relished the idea of all those paper houses burning up. Although a long time later I learned that little damage was done in that raid, we were pleased at the time because the Japs thought they could go everywhere and cause as much damage and suffering as they wanted to and their own homes would never be touched by the war. Well, Colonel Doolittle's bombers put them right on that idea. "Japan has been bombed!" Great stuff. But there wasn't much "great stuff" to cheer about in late spring and early summer, 1942.

Even Australia was preparing for an invasion and it looked as if nothing could stop the "Yellow Peril" as some folk called the Japanese, though I couldn't see the connection between them and pearls. The Jerries were winning in North Africa and then the Philippines surrendered to the Japanese. Everywhere, it was bad news.

Well, not quite. One of the heads of the German S.S. called Reinhard Heydrich, was killed by Czech agents, and the American navy was winning battles against the Japanese navy, in the Battle of the Coral Sea and the Battle of Midway, and in later years we were to see picters from Hollywood about these battles with John Wayne as big and brave as anything, and there was even a picter about Heydrich being killed, but that wasn't so good because the Jerries wiped out the village near where he was shot, all the men killed and the women and children sent to concentration camps. Not so good. But there was still more bad news. Tobruk was captured by Rommel! The gloom of the fall of Tobruk wasn't helped by RAF thousand bomber raids on Germany. Of all the defeats of the war, the fall of Tobruk seemed to hurt us most. Apart from St Valery. Even in Russia, the Jerries were advancing. I think that summer of 1942 was not a happy time to be listening to the nine o'clock news. And yet, looking back, I believe it was in that summer the tide of war began to turn in our favour.

And it was from that time I date my vertigo. I had been to see a picter called "The 49th Parallel". It was about a U-Boat crew landing up in the Arctic area of Canada and making their way to America, to New York in fact, and somehow, this villain of a Nazi was climbing about outside the torch of the State of Liberty and the G-man or FBI or maybe it was a Canadian Mounted Policeman in plain clothes was after him and the Nazi slipped and the hero grabbed him by the sleeve of his jacket to save him. You could see down past the Nazi to the ground far below, then you saw the stitching coming out that joined the sleeve to the jacket. I recall each frightening detail and that was nearly sixty years ago. The stitching came out and the hero was left holding an empty sleeve and you saw the screaming Nazi becoming smaller and smaller as he fell to the ground far below. By the way, I have since climbed with my wife to the top of the Statue of Liberty, though we weren't allowed up to the torch. We made do with looking out the windows in her crown and I looked down to the ground. I would like to say it cured my vertigo, but it hasn't.

In Peterhead's north harbour was the model jetty, and during the war, it was out of bounds, with a barbed wire barrier preventing access with armed guards at the gate. Why the security? Because it was the fitting-out base for the motor-torpedo boats which used to go on raids to Norway. My father worked on them and the unusual aspect of those MTBs, as they were called, was that after every few trips, their contents were emptied out and they were refitted as new. It was on one such occasion that one of their crew gave Father some ground coffee. He was a Norwegian and he visited us. We had never seen coffee before and we didn't know how to prepare it, but mother boiled it in a pot and we got a cup of it. What a taste! To me, it was electrifying. Maybe that's what made me the coffee-holic I am today, for as a bairn, I fell in love with it. Drinking coffee nowadays reminds me of that first taste.

And the books. Each MTB had its own small library, and they were dumped on the quay at refitting time for disposal to the scaffies. I was down the braes one evening with pals when mother shouted on me - father had books from an MTB. So I abandoned my friends and tore up to the house. The books had been rescued from the rubbish. I remember two of them - one was a small dictionary illustrated with line-drawings. It may have been used by Norwegian crewmen learning English.

Anyway it was discarded and I claimed it, and it went into my school bag. I remember one of its drawings - of figs growing on the tree. I loved that dictionary. The other book I treasure is one I never read, though I did start on its first paragraph. Its title was "The Bridge of San Luis Rey". But I never read it then because it was heavy going for a ten-years old, but I have read it since, as a sort of belated tribute to those brave Norwegian and British sailors who went over to Norway on those MTBs. I still found it heavy going though it said some good things about love and dying. I should have said the sailors were both British and Norwegian and in later years we learned they were working for our Secret Intelligence Service, which was why the Model Jetty base was a Very Restricted area.

Chapter 16

The fugitives

I was not long home from school, mother was in the scullery getting ready the evening meal, and I think my brother, Alex, was away to his after-school work as a message-boy with Bogies "the grocer". A normal quiet summer's day, and the War was far from my thoughts, though for the adults it was always there or thereabouts. There was a knock on the door at the top of the stairs. I ran to answer it.

What a shock. Two policemen at the door.

"Your mother or father in?"

"Mither," I called, "it's the Bobbies." And mother appeared from the scullery, drying her hands, apprehension etched on her face. Bad news, it had to be bad news.

"Mrs Davidson, it's about your son, William. Can we come in?" And without more ado, the two policemen walked along our lobby into the kitchen. So much for warrants and waiting until they were invited in and such-like.

"Fit's wrang?" Mother was scared to ask, but she had to know. I can just imagine what she must have thought. Something terrible happened to Willum, but when something bad happened, it wasn't the police who came, but a telegram boy with his yellow envelope. We'd seen it often enough to know how bad news was delivered from the government to your door. So what could these Bobbies be here for?

"Your son, William, in the army. Have you seen him recently?"

Mother was taken aback. "He's away in Wales somewhere. He moved down there from Orkney."

"He's not at his camp, Mrs Davidson. Him and his mate, Private McRobbie. They're on the run from the army."

By the way, I'm calling his mate: "Sandy McRobbie" though that is not his real name, because I haven't had his permission to write this, and the last we heard of him he was back in the Orkney with the Royal Artillery. He may not want me to tell his story so I'm concealing his identity. If he is still around and reads this, he'll understand why.

William and his pal, Sandy, had gone AWOL - Absent without leave - a serious offence in wartime, though not so bad as desertion. Why had he done it? The police didn't know. They just wanted to ask if we had seen him, one speaking to mother, and the other having an illegal look round the house. Illegal, because they had no warrant to search the house. But who was asking about warrants when mother was still in shock at hearing the Police were looking for our Willum.

They were satisfied the fugitives weren't at 14 Ives Park and left. And mother went back to preparing supper, in a state of shock. The shock continued when father came home from work, then Jess from the Woollen Mill, and Alex from Bogies. What a dismal supper that was. My Father shaking his head and repeating over and over: "At's affa at..." As an ex-soldier, he understood the enormity of going AWOL.

Then another knock at the door. Surely not the Bobbies back. I wasn't trusted to answer the door. Mother went. It was Aunt Muggie - one of Father's sisters - who lived across the road from us, on the Ugie Park side. She looked round the gloomy faces and asked: "Fit's wrang? Ye're affa doon in the mou.." So Father told her. There was no point in hiding it. The shameful secret had to be out, the Police were after Willum, and his pal, Sandy.

"An the Bobbies are lookin' a'wye for him and we dinna ken far he is. He's missin' - Absent without Leave," added Father, his familiarity with military terminology coming to his rescue.

Then Muggie dropped her bombshell. "He's ower in my back-bed-room..."

"Fit?" But he was. And it all came out. How Aunt Muggie had been through shopping in Aberdeen and seen Willum and another soldier down by Mealmarket Street, looking for someone they recognised from Peterhead, for Mealmarket Street was the Aberdeen terminus of the bus for Peterhead. And when she asked him what he was doing, he told her that he and Sandy were on the run and they were looking for the price of their fares to Peterhead. So she took them home and they got off the bus outside the town and walked the last mile or so by back streets. And now they were in her house having their supper.

What excitement. What pandemonium. And there was no possibility of turning them into the police. Late at night they came across to our house and moved into the back-bedroom, after they saw how they could escape down the drain-pipe if the Bobbies returned. And so began a fortnight or so of a bold cat-and-mouse game. The police did not look very hard for them. And even a military policeman who knew our family turned a blind eye. Willum and Sandy had gone into the North-Eastern (later renamed the Caledonian) bar for a pint, and there was the MP at the counter having a drink. He spotted Willum right away.

"Bill, what're you doing here? We're looking everywhere for you?"

"We're just in for a drink. You dinna see us." So the friendly MP turned back to his beer and by the time he turned round a few minutes later, the fugitives had gone.

Willum and Sandy went up to the McRobbie family for a few days - they lived round the Moray coast a bit - but Sandy's family were nervous about having them, so they visited our relatives in Buckie, and spent a few days in the Harbour Master's office, being looked after by our Auntie Lizzie Anne. Her man worked in the office. Then the bold heroes came back to Peterhead. One bonnie evening Willum and his girl-friend, Jeannie Youngson, whom he later married, went for a walk, and Jess and I took Sandy for a turn around the town. I remember walking along Station Road beside the cemetery wall and thinking, 'Fit wid we dee if the Bobbies catched us?" But they never did catch us.

Then on a Sunday evening - the last day they could be AWOL - if they were still on the run on the Monday they'd be charged with Desertion - or if they had got rid of their uniforms, that was also Desertion - on the Sunday evening, well-fed and smartened up, Willum and Sandy turned themselves in at the local police station. Within half an hour, the Bobbies were at our door, informing us our soldier son had given himself up and wanted to see his Father. So Father went down to the police station, and there in a cell, he shook his head at his wayward son and lamented over his behaviour.

"Can we not get out for a few minutes, just to visit my folks?" asked Willum. "We've come a' the wye from Wales and it's a shame we can't get to visit them." But no! They could not be released from custody. "You should have just visited your family before you turned yourself in," one of the friendly police advised them, but it was too late now. They were in custody, and they had to stay that way. Just as well, anyway, because if it had been another day, they would have been in bad trouble...

So why had they gone AWOL? There was a fanciful tale Willum told us - perhaps Sandy had a version tailored for his family. A story of being bored out of their skin up in Orkney looking after guns and wanting excitement so they volunteered for Special Services, and how Sandy could not stomach the parachute jumps, so rather than Willum continuing with this branch of the army and Sandy going back to the RA, they absconded. That was the story - all about close pals not wishing to be separated - but after 30 days in the "glass house" - the military prison at Colchester - they were separated anyway. Sandy was sent back to Orkney, and William was transferred into Lord Lovat's Commandos.

And that was the story I believed until Willum confessed the truth of the matter, on the evening of his eightieth birthday celebration. I'm not sure I am free to tell it even now, but it involves a local publican in Wales who dabbled in black-market meat, and a police search, and Willum convincing his pal that army detention centre was better than a civil prison, and a spur of the moment decision to disappear before the police returned. Enough said, though you can see why I haven't given Sandy McRobbie's real name. And two Canadian paratroops were also involved, but Willum never saw them again, either.

Sandy went to a different unit, and Willum lost touch with him. My brother went on to an adventurous life which is worth a book in itself. And for the Davidsons? We visited the McRobbie family and they visited us and there was a friendship, but eventually we lost contact. When the two sons of the families were no longer pals, there was nothing to hold the two families together. But I'm disappointed in a way, because we had a lot in common. I still have memories of the family, or rather of Sandy's two young brothers, one about my age and the other a few years my junior. We had visited them at their home in the country and on the Saturday evening, the brothers and I helped ourselves to cherries which grew over the wall of a nearby estate, then we chased rabbits, and actually trapped a baby rabbit in a jacket thrown by one of the boys. I wanted to keep it as a pet but they scoffed at the idea and released it. Then next day, Sunday, we went for a walk through the woods with our parents and the younger brother was rubbing at his arm with a stone and he turned and asked me: "Is 'at sair?" I was taken aback by the daftness of the question and answered, not very diplomatically: "I dinna ken. It's you that's gettin' it, nae me." A dig in the back from my Father reminded me that one should humour wee boys, especially when we were guests of his family.

Another memory of the younger McRobbie boys was when they came to Peterhead for the weekend. I was asked to take them "doon the Braes" on the Sunday afternoon. They wanted to learn how to catch fish, so I took my line with me, though I knew there would be no fishing that day because big waves were breaking over the rocks. But off we went to the Bogie Hole, though I warned them to keep well back because of the big seas.

"Fit div ye dee?" they asked. So I showed them. I broke off a limpet, fixed a piece of its hard flesh to the hook, and threw it out into the boiling waves of the Bogie Hole. My idea was to go through the motions of catching, though I had never heard of anyone trying to catch in those kind of seas. My intention was to keep it up for a few minutes then declare: "Nithin catchin' the day.." and go back up the road. But that is not how it worked out. I actually felt a tug on my line, so I ripped it, and there on the hook was a small podlie. I pulled it ashore to the amazed gasps of the McRobbie boys. "There wunna be ony mair noo," I announced, as if I knew all about the ways of fish. But they weren't wanting any more. They had their fish, and they bore it up the road to show their parents. They thought I was a great fisherman, but it was the flukiest catch I'd ever seen. I couldn't repeat it if I fished for a hundred years. And if they read this now, at least they'll know the truth of that wonderful catch that stormy Sunday afternoon in Peterhead.

I've often thought of the Peterhead Bobbies, and how they reacted to the two fugitives who were supposed to have slept in hedges and barns with little food and no chance to wash or change their clothes on their trek from Wales - what did the Bobbies make of these fugitives marching smartly into the police station, spotlessly clean, brasses shining and sharp creases in their uniforms and obviously having dined well while on the run? They must have smiled to themselves, because anything less like exhausted fugitives you could not imagine. So, like the friendly Military Policeman, I don't think the Bobbies were trying too hard to apprehend Willum and Sandy.

Willum had an unusual life as a Commando. He and Jeannie were married, and they moved into a guest-house in Hove, near Brighton. No barrack-rooms for Commandos, but smart Bed and Breakfast accommodation, with their wives living with them. And every afternoon, Willum and his comrades gathered at the harbour then set off to sea in small fast motor boats. They went out to sea every night. So Jerry spies could tell their bosses across the water that the Commandos had set off on a raiding mission, but usually it was just a run out to sea, then back to harbour in the early hours of the morning. So after a time, the spies, and I am sure there had been spies, stopped reporting the evening sorties of the Commando raiders.

Willum did go on Commando raids. He never gave us any details, though there was the time he and some other Commandos captured a Jerry radar post and took one of its officers back as a prisoner. Another time he went to a French port, famous as a holiday resort before the war. They rampaged through the town, attacking Jerries and doing all sorts of things he never spoke about. But he would not tell us the name of the town. Yet, in a way, he did reveal where he had been. He gave me one of those concertina fold-outs with small picture-views of a holiday resort you can buy from a newspaper kiosk, and he said he got it on the seafront of the French town they visited. They were holiday pictures of a town called Deauville.

When Hitler declared that all Commandos taken prisoner were to be shot as criminals, that was something more for mother to worry about, and it just backed up what we knew already, that the Jerries were a bad lot. It made us more determined than ever to beat the Nazis

So that was a momentous year. It was the year the Davidson family became "criminals" - harbouring a fugitive from the law. But strangely enough, we never felt like criminals. And with the attitude of the friendly MP, and even the police who never really bothered us after that first visit to our home, it was almost a game we were playing for a while, until our two heroes went back to face the music and get on with their real job of winning the war.

Chapter 17

The tide on the turn

It must have been the summer of 1942 that the barbed wire round the slit-trenches and the sand-bag gun emplacement at the brig was removed. It was a hazard to civilians, and especially to bairns, and it did not look as if the Jerries were going to visit us after all, in spite of what a visitor from London said when he spoke to the Peterhead Invasion Committee. Every town was expected to have an Invasion Committee whose main job was to keep us all prepared in case the Jerries did come. They had to make sure we knew what to do - to keep off the streets and not get in the way of our soldiers and not run away in case we blocked up the roads for our tanks and so forth. Anyway, that visitor said Hitler did not have "a dog's chance of winning this war unless he could successfully invade the British Isles." For British Isles, read Peterhead. But it also meant Hitler "did not have a dog's chance" - whatever that was - of winning the war because we knew he had enough on his plate with the Russians and our boys in North Africa. So we welcomed the removal of the barbed wire because it meant our soldiers knew there would be no invasion. And it also meant we could play in those wonderful trenches and the sand-bag machine-gun post

That summer and autumn we had many an evening invading Ives Park and being repulsed, or did the repelling, depending on whether we were Jerries or British. And sometimes we invaded Germany. What joy, to climb over that machine-gun post and shoot into the slit-windows. The sun shone and we got sand in our face and our clothes and our hair. And that sand reminds me of a significant rite of passage of my young life.

I'd been about ten years old - maybe still nine. Anyway, it was there or thereabouts. We were the invaders, and we were on top of the machine-gun place. Some of the sandbags were losing their contents, and were a good bit thinner. And as we prepared to burst in on the defenders down below, I had a mad idea which I immediately acted on - I threw a half-filled sandbag in through the window. What a mistake! Or was it? Because it hit a girl on the head, and she was about thirteen or fourteen years old. I should have mentioned earlier - girls fought alongside boys in those invasion battles, both for the invaders and the defenders. Anyway, I don't know how I found myself actually inside the emplacement, but there I was, and the girl was furious with all the sand in her hair and face, and she wanted to make me into mince-meat. I had to admit she was justified in her ambition. Her weight and fury drove me to the ground with her on top and she would have really minced me, especially since I'd lost the power in my hands. My strength drained away because as I put my hands up to hold her away, they touched her chest. She was soft and bumpy, and in that moment, I was paralysed by a new experience. The other boys and girls persuaded her not to commit murder, and reluctantly she desisted. Meanwhile, I simply gazed at her with open mouth. What was this new experience? I had just discovered that girls were very different from boys... in a nice kind of way. That was almost sixty years ago, and I still remember it very clearly...

While we were playing at fighting Jerries, bairns elsewhere were meeting Jerries in real life and it was no fun for them. Like the bairns at that town of Lidice where the S.S. man, Reinhard Heydrich, had been killed. The bairns there were shot or sent to concentration camps, and the lucky ones were given to German families scattered about Germany so they could be brought up to serve Hitler and his Third Reich. I wonder where they ended up. We were fortunate in Peterhead because we could play at British and Jerries, but there were so many other bairns for whom it was deadly serious.

There was a wee bit of excitement in the town that June when a prisoner escaped from Peterhead Prison. I don't know how anyone would dare try to escape because the warders - we never called them prison officers in those days - carried rifles. But a man did escape. He was soon caught, however, when he got a lift in a lorry because the police were searching all lorries and vehicles that went through Ellon. His name was Edward Gill and he belonged to something called the IRA. Although our parents probably knew what the IRA was, it meant nothing to bairns. If he'd been a Jerry now, we'd have understood, but IRA meant nothing to us.

That summer I gave my mother an affront. You see, it was school prize-giving, although there were no prizes, just certificates. Anyway, I knew I was to get a certificate but I didn't bother to mention it at home, and on the day of the certificate awards - the last day of school term - lots of the mothers were there to see their bairns march to the front to get their awards. But my mother didn't go, and more importantly, while other bairns wore their Sunday clothes to get their certificates, and boys mostly had their hair plastered down and wore ties, I went just with my usual clothes and a jersey and I suppose my hair was like a scare-crow. Mother nearly had a fit when I arrived home with my certificate. And of course father had to be told how she was affronted, though I think there was a bit of pride mixed in with it.

We could still get sweets in those days. Our ration was two ounces a week, which meant my brother, Alex, and I could manage a quarter of sweets between us. Jess, sent me up to Reid's shop once to get a quarter of sweeties, I think they were licorice allsorts, so I asked for "a quarter of an ounce." Barbara who served in the shop looked at me as if I was daft, but I assured her I had to get "a quarter of an ounce" so she measured it out and said not to bother with the sweetie coupon. Jess had a right laugh about it when I got home with the sweeties - I think there were two - and she and I had one each.

The nine o'clock news was grim that July. The Germans were still advancing, and our boys in North Africa had their backs to the wall in Egypt; and in Russia, it was said if the Jerries could capture a place called Stalingrad, they would win the war against Russia. And our Commandos made a disastrous attack on a place called Dieppe, where most of our men were either killed or taken prisoner, though some did make it back to Britain. Willum was not on that raid - in fact, he would have just been training to be a Commando at that time, up at a place near Spean Bridge. So although I can remember it as a lovely summer, it was bad news everywhere.

Hitler was still ranting on about the Jews. He must have had a thing about them. Like Heydrich, he had Jewish relatives, so maybe that was why he felt so bad about them. In one of his speeches he said: "I said that if Jewry started this war in order to overcome the Aryan people, then it would not be the Aryans but the Jews who would be exterminated. The Jews laughed at my prophecies ... I doubt if they are laughing now." When you hear Hitler saying that, you wonder if he was right in the head. We all knew Hitler started the war when he invaded Poland. Anyway, neither the Aryans nor the Jews were "exterminated", but it makes you wonder what kind of man it was that could speak so happily about human beings being "exterminated". You could speak about exterminating germs or vermin or garden-weeds, but not your fellow-men.

A nursery was opened in Windmill Street - it was called a Wartime Nursery, and its purpose was to allow mothers of small children go to work for the War Effort. It took all bairns from newly born infants up to five years of age, and I remember my sister, Jess, who was married to Sandy Watson by this time, taking her wee baby, Alan, to a Bonnie Baby Competition at the Nursery one Saturday. I could not believe it when Alan did not win the first prize. In fact, he did not win any prize. In my opinion, the judges were all daft and could not recognise a bonnie baby when they saw one. In later years, I revised my opinion of the judges, though I still think Alan should have won some prize. Perhaps, the happiest baby? But now I recognise the courage of anyone who judges a Bonniest Baby Competition. Personally, I have shied clear from any competitions where I would have to judge between babies, or dogs, or flowers or vegetables. Being a judge at such competitions calls for dedication and willingness for self-sacrifice way above the normal call of human duty.

Jess's husband, Sandy, was in the Royal Navy, and he often went on convoy duty to America. When he came on leave, he usually had a load of American comics with him. They were unlike any comics I had seen before - large thick-papered broad-sheets, with Lil Abner, Orphan Annie, the Lone Ranger and Tarzan of the Apes, and a host of other characters who seemed to epitomise the magic of America. That and the chocolate he brought home. And the cowboy magazines - with titles such as Western, Texas Ranger and Wild West. The thing about those comics and magazines was the smell they had - a new smell, of paper and print and something excitingly foreign.

About this time, a work-mate of my father, Davie Forbes, started visiting our home. Davie was the most well-read person I had ever met, though of course I didn't really know what "well-read" meant. I just knew that he had read so many books, and they were "good books". What I would recognise in later years as the classics. And when Davie saw me with my Western magazines, he said I should not waste my time reading them, but read books by writers such as Dickens and Walter Scott. I remember he recommended: "The Lay of the Last Minstrel". I think I must have been so over-awed by this man who knew so much about books that I decided to stop reading my Western magazines, and I never read another one, ever again. Davie had a son who was meant to go to University, but who had to go to the RAF and was now a belly-gunner in one of our big bombers. Then one day father came home from work and told mother how Davie's son had been killed coming back from a bombing raid.

Apparently, when his plane was about to land on its airfield in England, another plane was taking off, and they collided. Davie was shattered. I think his son was all the family he had, and the war had taken the boy from him. When father was describing to mother and another visitor Davie's reaction, I was taking it all in and I was so nervous at what my father was saying that I giggled. What a row I got! But mother calmed father down. "The bairn's nae meanin' tae be funny..!" And that is true. I was actually shocked by the depiction of a man, and especially Davie Forbes, crying.

After hearing about Davie's son, I suppose it meant a lot to see the film: "One of our aircraft is missing". There are few films I can remember from the war years, but that is one of them. I don't remember anything about the escape of the crew from Occupied Europe, but I do have a picture in my mind of the aircrew inside the bomber as it flies to Germany. It was such a dark and cluttered space inside the plane, and I could imagine the Forbes lad as he went off on his bombing raids.

That was the picters, though it reflected real life. Meanwhile, the Jerries were running out of steam in Russia, and the snow was starting to fall at Stalingrad. It was October, and the great Eighth Army offensive at El Alamein was just beginning, and it was going eventually to end up with all the Jerries and Italians kicked out of Africa, or taken prisoner. Even the Japs were beginning to suffer, and in New Guinea and islands around the Pacific, our boys, and that included American and Australian and New Zealanders as well as British servicemen, were beginning to score up victories on land, at sea and in the air. But there was no easy victory anywhere. The enemy were fighting desperately as they felt the tide of war beginning to flow more strongly against them. The nine o'clock news was more cheery now. And our big bombing raids on Germany - a thousand or more bombers at a time bombing one city - were beginning to hurt the German Home Front. When I first went into the RAF for my National Service, I remember having a lecture on the fire-storms of Hamburg and Bremen and other German cities. In a fire-storm there is so much fire in the centre of the city it causes an updraft like a gale and sucks all the oxygen out of the area so that people were suffocated rather than burned to death. War is a horrible experience, whether you're dishing it out or receiving it. Hitler with all his ranting, and Goering with his promises that Germany would never get bombed, were facing their doom, if they only knew it. If they had any sense at all, they must have known, as the winter of 1942/43 approached.

Chapter 18

Twilight of childhood

Every time Sandy came home on leave from the Navy he had American comics with him, but there was one time he hadn't. I think it was in December, 1942. And he had been on a liner-cum-troopship, the *Karanja*, landing troops in the North African landings, during Operation "Torch" as it was called. And of the ten ships in his convoy, eight were sunk by Stuka dive-bombers. His ship was one of the eight. Sandy was picked up by a cruiser and transferred to the liner, *Strathnaver*, which returned to Greenock with 500 survivors from various boats. He didn't have time to think of comics or anything else. In fact, all he owned on that trip to Greenock was a boiler suit and a pair of "jimmies" - not even socks. When he was kitted out, he got leave, before going back to another ship. But since we had never been informed of his ship being bombed from beneath him, we only learned of his close thing when he came home and told us. Anyway, it was a happy home-coming, even without the comics.

But Operation "Torch" was a success, and the Germans and the Italians were now caught between Montgomery's Eighth Army chasing Rommel from Egypt, and the British and American and French soldiers attacking him from behind in the west. Meanwhile, the Japs were putting up fierce resistance in the Pacific and the Germans were fighting like grim death in Russia, but gradually our enemies were being worn down. That is one thing about them, when they knew they were being gradually defeated, all of them - Jerries, Italians and Japs - they were putting up a tremendous resistance, especially the Japs. The only way we could defeat them was to kill or wound them all. They were refusing to surrender. And in Stalingrad, when the Jerries did not have a hope of winning because they were surrounded by Russian armies, they kept on fighting, even when they were starving. In fact, Hitler ordered them to fight to the last man and the last round of ammunition. When they did eventually surrender, at the end of January, 1943, it did not do them much good because the Russians made them march in the dead of winter all the way to Siberia to their POW camps, and many of the German prisoners died on the way. But if that was a bad thing for the Russians to do their German prisoners, it was no worse than the Germans did to their Russian prisoners. Willum was with the Commandos who liberated in 1945 a German camp for Russian women POWs up beside the Baltic Sea. He told us of how those women suffered at the hands of the Germans, though they did get their own back on their guards after they were freed - but that is not part of this story.

A new word entered our vocabulary about that time. "Harakiri". It seemed that Japanese officers committed harakiri rather than surrender, and this was to push their long swords up through their stomachs to their heart and lungs. We boys thought this was an attractive idea and we went through the motions of harakiri, using our school rulers. Needless to say, it was a temporary phase and it wasn't long before there was something else to take our attention.

"The Ghost of Frankenstein" was on at the picters and my sister, Jess, persuaded mother to go with her to see it, and they went, accompanied by Willum's wife, Jeannie, to take their minds off the war and the worries about their men. Jess and Jeannie were terrified at the monster and hid their faces most of the time, but they were amazed at my mother who just sat watching the antics on the screen, completely unmoved. When they came home they were telling us how mother wasn't in the slightest bit afraid of the Frankenstein monster, then mother explained why she wasn't "feart", and her response went down in the historical anecdotes of the Davidsons: "Fit wis there to be feart o' - it wis jist a mannie dressed up!" She was a very down-to-earth lady, perhaps reflecting her Cairnbulg background.

About this time a story went round the town about Bob the Baker's daughter, a missionary in China. Bob the Baker's shop was at the corner of Ugie Road and Skelton Street, just beside the bus-stop for the Broch and Macduff and Buckie, if you were going there. I say that because we sometimes went to Buckie to see relatives and that is the bus-stop we left from. It was just across from Chipper Elsie's. Now, that was some chip shop, though I didn't realise it at the time. In those days, well 1939 and 1940, really, you could get a bag of chips for one penny. We used to collect lemonade and beer bottles and take them down to Hunter's Brewery in Tanfield Close, where the car park is nowadays opposite the Broo, where we exchanged bottles for money to buy chips.

It was a happy experience to visit Chipper Elsie's for a bag of chips and a small bottle of lemonade - everything was called either "lemonade" or "A1", regardless of the flavour, whether it was orange or strawberry or whatever - anyway, Chipper Elsie had a special bag of chips for us bairns - a half-penny bag. It was a penny bag cut to only half the height of a penny bag, and we could afford a half-penny bag when we couldn't afford a penny. Of course, you didn't get a lot of chips for your halfpenny, but we didn't need a lot, because we weren't hungry - it was just the thought of having a bag of chips. Chipper Elsie's was the only shop in the town that gave you a half-penny bag, and I cherish her memory for her kindness to the bairns from nearby streets.

Anyway, the word was that Bob the Baker's daughter, Annie Buchan, who was matron at a missionary hospital away somewhere in China where the Japanese were, was safe and well, and working with her - I think he was a doctor - was Eric Liddell, the famous Scottish Olympic runner. Now that was something, a Buchanhaven quine with a famous sportsman and looking after all those sick and wounded in the middle of China, and the Japanese soldiers there, but she would not run away and leave her patients. If she could put up with that, we could put up with the war and the blackouts and the worry of our loved ones at the Battle Front, wherever they were. Though you have to admit it was very difficult for those who were visited by the telegram boy with his dreaded yellow envelope.

Every week or so a new crime was reported. The most common one was people leaving their job without permission from the government. If you were in a job important to the War Effort, you were stuck in it, and if you left you could be up in court and fined. But the most unusual crime just then was a wifey who was separated from her man down in England and she came back home to Peterhead to live. She didn't want to have her married name any more because she was finished with her man, so she rubbed out her married name on her identity card and wrote her own family name on it. I suppose, in time of war with the fear of spies going about, that was a daft thing to do, although she meant no harm. Anyway, the sheriff thought it a serious enough crime, and she was fined £1. If I remember correctly, we all had ID cards, but I haven't seen my one for years. I can remember it's number, however: SWOA 16.5.

That winter must have seen the last of the big crowd of the Blinner loons, because most of the older ones were about to leave or had just left school. You left school at fourteen in those days, and most of the boys from round the doors left school as soon as possible and went to work as message boys with shops or in Dickie's Sawmill, until they could get taken on as an apprentice to learn a trade. Ch-harging was a thing of the past, and the nearest we got to it was Big hannie-oot. Big hannie-oot was ordinary hannie-oot, but on a bigger, town-wide scale. Hannie-oot involved two sides, one catching, and the other running free. The idea was to run between two "barlies" or dens, usually a gate at each end of the road, and the side who were "oot" or free had to do the running, and the other side had to do the catching. If you were caught, you went into another "barlie", and you had to stay there until one of your team touched you and set you free. Of course, there were usually one or two guards at the prisoner "barlie", and it wasn't easy to get freed. And Big hannie-oot was this same game, except that while the "barlies" were still there, you did not have to run directly between the two designated ones, but you could run free all round the town and it was possible to be running for a whole evening while the catchers looked for you. But I must say I did not think much of it as a game, and there were occasions when someone who had been caught, or even their guards, got fed up and went home without ever seeing any more of the two sides for the rest of the evening.

In those last days of the big crowd, one or two events stand out in my memory. One of our number had heard about David and his sling killing Goliath, so he made a sling. I won't reveal his name, he is no longer with us, but he made that sling, the only one I ever saw fired in anger. He used it to fire big stones that filled your "niv" or hand. On one occasion at the bottom of our street he was demonstrating it, intending to throw a big stone far out past the mountainie, as we called the Ive Rock. But he misjudged, and the stone shot like a bullet away at a right angle to where it was supposed to go, and it went through the frosted glass in a wifey's door. What a crash! It was like a bomb going off. We couldn't run, there was nowhere to run. And our companion of the sling owned up, and his father duly fitted a new pane of glass in the door. He had the sling, but it had to be used doon the braes only, nowhere near houses. And you would think there would be no more trouble. But unfortunately, that was not the case.

We were right down below an overhanging cliff, below where the concrete gun-shelter was, half-way along to the cable-hoosie, and our sling-shot hero was bombarding scurdies and deuks out past the bogie-hole. Stones from that sling went an amazing distance. Unfortunately, one of his stones behaved erratically and flew up and high back over our heads. That was a shock, but there was more to come. A bobbie appeared within the hour and informed us a window had been broken. Did we do it? We protested innocence, pointing out it was physically impossible for us to throw a stone a way up the brae and past the overhang, and through a window about two hundred yards away. And the bobby reluctantly accepted the logic of that statement. Even the wifey whose window was broken had to accept it, though she still had her suspicions. I still don't know for sure who did it, though I suspect our sling-shot hero was the guilty one. Looking back, I believe he could have rivalled the shepherd-lad David and even brought Goliath down. But like David and Goliath, he is no longer with us, nor is the lady with the broken window, so that mystery will remain unsolved this side of time.

And another activity of those last days of the crowd in the Blinner was flying our kites. There were some beauties on display, made of barrel hoops and string and newspaper and floury paste. We could make kites which zoomed high in the sky, and I remember one, belonging to the sling-shot hero, which was away high up and far out to sea with a few balls of string joined together. And what a tragedy! The string snapped, and we could only watch in dismay as that beautiful big kite side-slipped far out into the North Sea. But there was no problem about making another kite. We all had them, and they were a refreshing change from playing at invasions and fighting Jerries, because the Jerries were never going to come. Instead, all the talk was about when we were going to invade them.

In the early hours one Saturday in February,1942, Jerry bombers visited Peterhead and the Broch. They dropped three bombs on Peterhead but they were a new kind of bomb, delayed action bombs, and they were supposed to blow up hours after they landed. No damage was done before they were defused but people had to be moved out of their houses nearby, though just for the night. The one that drew most comment was the one that landed in the foyer of the **Regal** cinema. It was discovered when a fire-watcher fell over it in the dark. But the Broch was not so fortunate. High explosive bombs were dropped there and much damage was done, there were casualties, and one eleven-year-old boy, Laurence Kerry, was killed when the house fell on top of him in bed. But Aberdeen suffered much worse the following year.

In April, 1943, Aberdeen was bombed and ninety-eight civilians were killed in one night, fifteen of them bairns aged ten and under, and 27 soldiers at the barracks. Whole families were wiped out, one of them the mother and father, and their four children. Long after the war one of the Luftwaffe crew on the raid revealed in a magazine it was a reprisal raid intended to boost the German public's morale. About forty Dornier two-engined bombers had been sent from their airfield near Utrecht in Holland up to Stavanger in Norway for the raid.

The bombers crossed the coast north of Aberdeen and approached the city just above roof-top height, dropping bombs and using machine-gun and cannon fire to do as much damage as possible. They were very pleased they managed to destroy a flak-tower before it could open fire on them, but the reason it didn't open fire was because it wasn't an anti-aircraft gun tower. It was the water-tower on top of the Co-op dairy on Berryden Road. Among the dead was a Mrs Forsyth and her baby son, Francis, killed when a cannon-shell ripped their roof off, and a Mr Webster, who was a veteran of the South African War. He had shepherded his family to safety out of their tenement house, then went back in to get his boots. A bomb hit the building and he was found later on top of rubble, dead.

The Jerries were relieved they suffered no casualties because raids on Britain had become almost suicide missions. Our authorities were taken completely by surprise and the enemy had their morale boost, though they did exaggerate the extent of their success.

That same night, bombers dropped bombs in fields outside Peterhead and the Broch, but there were no casualties, no damage done, apart from tiles blown off the roof of a cottar house. So it showed that although the worst of the bombing raids was over, the Luftwaffe could still exact a heavy toll on the folk of the north-east. In fact, the Lord Mayor of London gave money for relief in Aberdeen from the City of London Air Raid fund. Yet we knew the raids on us were small compared to the RAF thousand bomber raids on German cities.

Back to 1942, and the spring of that year saw the death of the mannie the bairns were afraid of, John Willox, the town's housing inspector who kept an eye on the council houses and their gardens, and especially the fences. We did pinch a few lathes off the fences for our swords, especially when "Zorro" was on at the picters, but we made sure that "Wullicks" didn't see our swords. But with his going, so passed an era in our childhood. It would never be the same again, although we didn't realise it at the time.

"Desert Victory" came to the picters, the **Playhouse**. And for about twenty minutes, our eyes and ears were bombarded with the sounds and flashes of the barrage of the Allied guns which started the battle of El Alamein, and eventually led to the defeat of Germany and Italy in North Africa. A joke went round that an American soldier wandered into a cinema in London and saw "Desert Victory" by mistake, and he got the Purple Heart medal for his courage. It's funny how we poke fun at others, even our Allies, and it was very unjustified. In fact, after the war, as we got to know the truth about all the battle fronts, it was obvious that every side had its heroes and its cowards, and that most serviceman and women, no matter whether friend or foe, fought bravely. I suspect they fought with more courage and loyalty than the leaders who got us into the war deserved. That opinion, however, was for long after the war. In 1943, it was total war, and that could include character as well as physical assassination.

Chapter 19

Good and Bad News

War Savings was a big thing on the Home Front. All the time, in the newspapers and on the radio and in posters stuck up everywhere, we were called upon to save money for the War Effort. On Monday mornings we took our pennies and three-penny bits and even sixpences to school where the teacher collected them and wrote our name down in a register, and after a time when the money accumulated, we were given a War Savings Certificate. The figure that sticks in my head about those certificates is they were worth fifteen shillings - about 75pence nowadays. Not a lot you may surmise, but when you remember that Loan Companies were offering loans from £5 to £500, money was worth a lot more in those days. Everybody, well almost everybody, was saving money as a means of helping to beat the Jerries. I know my parents had a book of certificates and after a time we received an illuminated letter of thanks from the King for saving so much money, and it was framed and put up on the wall. There were campaigns to raise money for the RAF - ""Wings for Victory" Week - was one of them, and towns were given a target-figure they were supposed to raise . Peterhead and the Broch were each given a similar target, £75,000; the combined total of £150,000 to raise in one week from the peacetime population of the two towns of about 25,000 people, men, women and bairns, was a hefty target, especially when you remember the small wages people were getting at that time. But the targets weren't too high for us, because Peterhead raised just over £150,000, and the Broch achieved almost £130,000. Then there were campaigns to raise money for warships, and for guns and to help the Russians. During the time of the Normandy landings there was a "Salute the Soldiers" Week, and the Broch and Peterhead were given the same targets again. Saving was very much a part of winning the War and it went on non-stop.

There were campaigns to collect metal for guns and planes and shells. Iron railings and gates went for the War Effort, and aluminium pots and pans and kettles were contributed because aluminium was used to make Spitfires and other warplanes. Books were collected for "our boys" at the front or on convoys and warm clothing was donated and balaclavas knitted, especially for the Russian front or our convoys going to Murmansk and Archangel. Anything and everything that could be used for scrap was collected and sent off to help the War Effort. Total war meant not only that civilians could be killed by enemy action, but also that civilians had a contribution to make in killing the enemy. It must have been a difficult time for pacifists or conscientious objectors. It was easier to go with the tide of the corporate blood lust. And that wasn't too difficult when all the time you were hearing of our people being killed by the Jerries or the Japs, soldiers, sailors, airmen, both men and women, and civilians in their own homes. Nowhere was out of bounds for Nazi bombs. So we did all we could to get our own back and kill them for what they were doing to us.

We never went hungry in the war. Much food we liked was missing. Fresh eggs was a luxury, and what we got was dried or powdered eggs. Powdered eggs was very good for baking, and when it was beaten up with a drop of milk, it made a passable omelette or could pass for fried egg, all yellow, no white, and all solid. If you were hoping for something that looked like a fried egg you were disappointed, but if you were merely looking for something both filling and edible, then you'd be satisfied.

And fruit - apart from that surfeit of Canadian MacReds from the bombed ship - fruit was always in short supply. Bananas were non-existent. There was a story in the *Sunday Post* about a boy in Glasgow who was very ill and he needed bananas - doctors' orders, it seems - and an appeal went out for bananas, and someone who had brought bananas home on leave from abroad, gave up his fruit to the sick child. There was even a song about bananas: "Yes, we have no bananas - we have no bananas today!" It was a pre-war song from America, but for a while it was a theme song to highlight the shortages of those days:

> "Yes, we have no bananas
> We have no bananas today.
> We've string beans, and onions,
> And corns and bunions
> And all sorts of fruit and say
> We have an old fashioned tomata
> A New Jersey potata
> But, yes, we have no bananas.
> We have no bananas today!"

Those were not the words of the original song because it used American terms such as "cabashes" and "scallions", and I'm sure it didn't mention "corns and bunions" but we weren't slow to adapt if we wanted to fit in our own words. Recently I tried to find the words used in the Backie Concerts, but memories are getting sketchy and many of the older folk who would have known the words are not with us any-more.

During a raid in April a Peterhead man's lum went on fire and he and another man climbed up on the roof and put the fire out with a bag. But an ARP Warden spotted him and he was hauled up in court and fined twenty-five shillings for "displaying a light from his chimney." I think that was the night Aberdeen was badly bombed, but the only bombs near Peterhead landed in a field out in the country somewhere. Our mothers knew what they were doing when they set our chimneys on fire during daylight hours. It saved them money in fines and even the cost of chim-ney sweeps, and it allowed us to bank up the fires on those cold wintry nights when the wind roared in the lum without the fear of "displaying a light" from our chimney.

One bit of good news that summer was that Jimmy Stewart, the neigh-bour's son who was missing when his ship was sunk by the Japs the pre-vious year was now reported as a prisoner of war. But there was bad news. Especially about the two wee brothers, Harry and Tommy Rose who lived Ower the Queenie, who were both drowned in the South Harbour. Even today, those who were in Peterhead at that time can remember the shock of those drownings. Another death announced that summer was the news that the famous Japanese Admiral Yamamoto who was in charge of their forces in the Pacific was in a plane shot down by American fighters. That helped to make up for all the bad news we had in the war against the Japanese and cheered us up a bit. But in the sum-mer of 1943, there was fierce fighting on all the different war fronts. Almost everywhere the enemy was being beaten back, and the fighting in North Africa had finished when the enemy finally surrendered there.

German cities were being pulverised by thousand bomber raids, and dams which supplied Germany with electricity were bombed. We heard on the news that lots of their land and homes and factories were flooded by the water from the breached dams. It sounded good and was a great morale booster, and in later years they even made a film of it, but it sounded better than it really was. In fact, it didn't take the Jerries long to repair the dams. But it was all part of the general news that we were win-ning the war and it was only a matter of time to victory, in those exciting days of the summer of 1943. But there was still a long way to go, and there were still those yellow envelopes being delivered by the telegram boys.

I can remember one of those yellow envelopes, though I did not see it delivered. One of our neighbours' daughters had married a French Canadian soldier. A great guy, he was, and they had two small daugh-ters. One Sunday evening, early in 1943, I think it was, I visited them.

The soldier was home on leave, and the whole family were gathered round the kitchen table, playing Monopoly. I had never seen this game before, and I was intrigued with it. So the soldier, lets call him Pierre, though that was not his real name, asked me to help him. So I stood beside him and threw his dice, and helped to move his piece round the board. I can remember that game so clearly. Pierre didn't win, but I think he managed not to go to jail. Anyway, the next day, or soon afterwards, Pierre went back to his unit, then we heard that the Allies had invaded Sicily. The Canadian army was in that invasion. Pierre was part of that invasion. We were winning, and the Jerries and the Eyeties were getting beat, and it was an exciting summer, the summer of 1943. Until word came - one of those horrible yellow envelopes. Pierre had died in action in Sicily. Much later, we heard how it happened. He had been wounded, and was being taken back from the front in an ambulance, to a hospital out of harm's way. And a shell, or it may have been a bomb, hit the ambulance. And Pierre, he of the heroic dark hair and eyes and the ready grin, had been killed by the Jerries at their second attempt. I was sad about Pierre being killed, though I had really only met him the once. The world was a poorer place for the loss of that dashing French Canadian. But when I think of it, Pierre and his death, was repeated thousands and thousands of times. So I found it easy to decide that war was bad! A profound conclusion for a ten-years-old philosopher.

It was no consolation to hear that more bombs had been dropped on Hamburg in one night than the combined weight of bombs dropped on London in the five worst raids it had encountered. And when we heard that 20,000 Germans had been killed in that city in one night, and 60,000 injured, it made less impression on me and the people of Peterhead than the loss of the two wee Rose boys in the harbour. Maybe some folk would condemn us for our lack of sense of proportion, but that was the mood in Peterhead in those days. But having said that, the impact our bombing raids were having was brought home to us in an exhibition put on by the RAF in the Central School, showing high-level photographs of German and Italian cities after they had been visited by our bombers. Not a pretty sight, even if they were enemy cities.

Then came the news: Mussolini had been sacked! He was under arrest. What did Churchill call him? A jackal? Anyway, it served Mussolini right! But I could not understand how the Italians could cheer him on when things were going great for them, then turn against him when things were going badly. A long time later I heard that Mussolini had said at the time: "A war that goes badly is one man's war, but they are the people's wars when ... they end in victory." I know that some Italian soldiers were very brave in North Africa, but I can not say I respected the Italians for the way they turned against their own leader. And I was only a bairn at the time. The ten-years-old - no, an eleven-years-old - philosopher by the autumn of 1943, had formed an opinion of a whole nation with no help from anyone. In fact, on the day of my eleventh birthday, American planes bombed Rome for the first time, though not where the Pope lived, and it was a shock to the morale of the Italian people. It was all on the radio news the next day. And that served the Italians right! That summer was a time of "served them rights", especially for Hitler and the Jerries in Russia where their Panzer corps were nearly wiped out in the battle of Kursk, at what was called the greatest tank battle ever. And the Japs were getting their just desserts in the Pacific, though they were still fighting like grim death, and the only way to defeat them was to kill them, because they never surrendered. And in Sicily, we were winning and pushing the Jerries and Italians back into the sea. Patton and Montgomery were the American and British generals! Our heroes, though afterwards we heard they couldn't stand the sight of each other.

Then came the invasion of Italy and the writing was on the wall for the Axis. I can use that word now but I wouldn't have recognised it then. If anyone had asked us bairns about the Axis, we would have said they were for chapping firewood. Italy surrendered, then declared war on Germany, but we weren't impressed. The Russians now - they were brilliant, knocking the Jerries to bits. And the Japs, they were daft. They were getting beat, but rather than surrender, they used to blow themselves up with hand-grenades. Come to think of it, we heard of German and Italian prisoners of war, but never Japanese prisoners of war. There must have been some, but not so as you'd notice. In fact, it was said that the word "surrender" was not in their language, though that was hard to believe. And that winter of 1943, the German battleship *Scharnhorst* was sunk as she was trying to attack one of our convoys to Russia. Things were going badly for Adolf Schickelgruber.

Something that came back to me recently, and it seems ironic to me now, but I never thought so as a bairn, was that during the War, we still held Armistice Day. I can remember sitting with arms folded in class as we reached the eleventh hour on the eleventh day of the eleventh month - November. Armistice Day! And the silence that fell. Towards the end of the war, even Dickie's Sawmill went silent for a minute or two, and that was a constant noise all my school days. Thump! Thump! Thump! You never noticed it until it stopped, and it went silent at Armistice time. But how could the powers-that-be justify an Armistice Remembrance when a new war had broken out between the countries which had held the Armistice in the first place? The answer was probably because we were remembering the dead. Of the First War - or both World Wars?

What about the enemy dead? There were almost 2,000 men on the *Scharnhorst* alone and less than forty of them survived. We would not remember them. No! They were enemy, and they didn't count. If anything, we rejoiced over them being dead. So we thought of people we knew who had been killed and did what Mr Mair, the headmaster, told us to do and sat in silence with arms folded.

Our worst complaint that winter - apart from the dread of a yellow envelope being delivered to our door, and that dread was always with us - was that we were not getting extra sweetie coupons for Hogmnay. For some reason - and we bairns were not mollified - dried peas were coming off the ration and we could get as many "wrinkly peas" as we wanted. But not extra sweets. "Ah, well," we had to console ourselves, " - there's a war on!" And I must admit I did enjoy boiled peas.

Chapter 20

Victory

An air of expectancy ushered in 1944. The enemy was as thrawn as ever with his back to the wall, whether it was the Japs or the Jerries. It seemed our forces were advancing everywhere, but it was two steps forward and one back. As far as Buchan was concerned, we were not having the bombing raids of the past, though there was the occasional sortie by the Luftwaffe, usually coming across to machine-gun towns and villages. Most of their aerial power was thrown against the Russians and our lads in Italy, or getting ready for the Allied invasion of Hitler's Atlantic Wall along the coastline of France. War was getting less irksome for us. No longer did we look for an invasion, the shoe was on the other foot. And convoys were not being bombed off the coast so there were less air-raid sirens. In April, oranges were on sale in the shops, a pound in weight for each ration book. That was a good sign we were winning the war. I'm sure the Germans weren't getting oranges.

That spring I had an unexpected find when I was beach-combing down the braes - I was "scranning", as we called it. It was a Saturday morning and a wet sun glinted off the rocks after a week of gales and stormy seas. In a rock pool I found two large boxes strung together by rope with their lids tied down. They had obviously been washed in by the big seas. Close examination showed they were full of lobsters, alive and rustling. There was no means of identifying ownership so I went up to the house and our downstairs neighbour, Jimmy Hamilton, who was my senior by about five years, came back down with me and together, we carried the boxes up to our houses. Jimmy took one box, and I the other. I don't know what I was going to do with our lobsters, but they ended up in a cupboard at the top of the stairs. Their big pincers were tied so they were harmless, but on one occasion when the cupboard door swung open, I was faced with a phalanx of lobsters with waving antennae crawling along the lobby towards the kitchen. No one wanted cooked lobster in our house, so the Davidson's lobsters eventually ended up - with claws untied - back in the Bogey Hole. There must have been an unexplained surge in the lobster population in the neighbourhood, and anyone with a lobster creel would have had a temporary bonanza.

There was even more bad feeling against the Germans when we heard about the Great Escape, as it was called, when a large number of British and Commonwealth airmen were caught after escaping from a prisoner of war camp, and almost fifty of them were shot by the Gestapo. It was on the news, but what made it worse for Peterhead was that one of the Canadian airmen shot was the nephew of a Peterhead man whose brother had emigrated to Canada before the First World War. He was the lad Wernham, whose uncle had a newsagent shop in Broad Street. It incensed us even more against the Jerries. So we were all the more pleased when a few weeks later, in June, it was on the radio that units of an Allied invasion force had been landing on the coast of Normandy during the night. Great! Now we were really winning, and it was only a matter of time. But it was worrying, too. Because we knew that Willum and the Commandos would be in the thick of it, and it later proved right. He was "in the thick of it", having landed not too far from Deauville, the town he visited earlier in the war.

There was no word of him, but no news was good news. We didn't want word of him, we did not want one of those yellow telegram envelopes coming to our door. And with each passing week and no news of how he was doing meant he was probably still all right. But casualties were mounting up, wounded and killed, there was a never-ending stream of notices in the newspapers. And to break the tension of that summer, my parents decided to have a holiday with relatives at Buckie, which was our normal holiday resort, stopping off for a day at another friend's house near Banff. We arrived at Buckie on the Friday afternoon, only to be greeted by a yellow telegram envelope, sent from Peterhead. What could it be? It took a lot of courage for mother to open that envelope, but there was no point in delaying it.

And what a relief! Willum was back in this country on leave from the front and would be home in Peterhead on Monday. We learned later that his Commando had been nearly wiped out near Caen and the remnant had come back to the UK to regroup and become part of a replacement Nº 6 Commando. He was one of the twenty or so per cent unscathed survivors. The rest were either wounded or killed.

Thinking back to the autumn of 1944, there was an almost dream-like quality to those days, because it was obvious we were winning the war, but there was also a feeling of something akin to impatience for the inevitable victory to happen. And our casualties figures were mounting up and up. The invasion was proving very costly, but we were winning, though it wasn't victory all the way. There were set-backs - such as the disastrous paratroop landings at Arnhem. Montgomery made a mistake there, or so we thought. One of the neighbours' sons was taken prisoner at Arnhem but he came home alive and well after the War. It seemed so out of order, that we were winning, yet we were losing so many men, taken prisoner, wounded or killed. Why couldn't the Germans see they were going to lose, and the only sensible thing would be to surrender and save lives. But then, our armies would have probably done the same if the Jerries had invaded us back in 1940. And the Japanese, they would resist even more.

The winter of 1944/45 was very stormy. In Europe, the Germans battered their way with the help of bad weather, through the American lines in the Ardennes and nearly made it to the town of Antwerp in Belgium. Then a combination of Allied resistance and the Jerries running out of fuel for their Panzers and an improvement in the weather allowing our air forces to attack them from the air, slowed them down and eventually put them to flight. Willum spent a week or so along with his fellow-commandos in landing barges off the Belgium coast held back in reserve in case the Jerries broke through to Antwerp. But that German offensive proved to be them shooting their last bolt. They didn't have much resistance after that.

Well, not quite true, because Hitler still had his secret weapons, his V1 and V2 rockets. We never had them in Scotland, they were aimed mostly at London, but I remember hearing one on the news - a recording of a V1 doodle-bug as it crossed London, then its engine cut-out, and the silence before the explosion. They were bad, but the V2 was worse. It fell from the edge of space, a huge silent rocket with an enormous amount of high-explosive on board.

Peterhead and the Broch were cut off from the outside world for about a fortnight by the snows of January, 1945. It got so bad, that an emergency transport service was set up by means of a drifter sailing between Peterhead and Aberdeen. It was only for real emergencies, or for servicemen going back from leave. About that time, after the Ardennes emergency was over, Willum was given leave again. And while at home and as the end of his leave approached, he went to the doctor's with what he thought was bronchitis, something contracted in his landing-barge off Antwerp. But the doctor - I think it was a gentleman named Dr Wooley - a bit stoutish and a real toff, and I remember him coming into our kitchen and standing with his back to fire, getting a heat - he decided Willum had congestion of the lungs. So the doctor sent him up to the Cottage Hospital for treatment. Willum was delighted, because although he was an in-patient, he was allowed out for a while during the day. So he got another week or two at home, but eventually he had to go back to the war, and our worries began again.

The winter was a bit stormy for me, too, because I eventually turned on a class-mate who had been trying to bully me for months. It was in

Mr Mair's class and I had taken as much as I was going to take from this lad's snide remarks, so I gave him some back, and it was all fixed up - just like that - we would fight it out down the laney after school. So come four o'clock, the two of us, with a class-mate to hold our bags and jackets, started our battle. We fought and punched each other for about half an hour, then a young man - he had been in his late teens - came down the lane on his way into town and lectured us on how foolish it was for us to fight. We listened sullenly, and as soon as he continued on his way, we continued the fight. About twenty minutes later he returned - he'd been shopping - and again he counselled us not to fight. This time, his words of wisdom fell on more receptive ears, because both of us were tired and finding it difficult to lift our arms.

"A' richt. We'll finish this fecht the morn!"

"Right! Here again, efter school!"

"Right!" And so we broke off hostilities and went our separate ways, content to finish our fight another day.

I should explain, although this class-mate and I never got on, nevertheless, there was an understanding between us: in English, when we were parsing sentences, I could look over his shoulder because he was good at that and I wasn't. While in algebra, I could do equations, and he couldn't, so he always sat behind me in maths to see my answers. We were far from being friends, but each of us found it convenient to co-operate in these academic matters. So next afternoon, in Miss Peterkin's algebra class, I was very aware of him craning his neck to see my answers, and I was not going to let him because there was still a fight to settle come bell-time. But he was making so much rustling and creaking his desk as he fidgeted about trying to get a sight of my pages, that I impulsively whipped round and stuck my jotter under his nose. He looked shocked, then burst out laughing. I couldn't help it, so did I.

When Miss Peterkin turned round from the black-board, we were sitting primly facing the front, trying hard to keep our laughter in. She was a good sort, and she just smiled and said something about our being happy at our studies. That fight after school never took place. On the contrary, my class-mate and I became firm friends, and so we continued until National Service separated us, and after the forces, we were both courting girl-friends, and had other interests, which did not include old school-pals. Though I always thought of him as a friend, and I made a point of attending his funeral some years ago. It just goes to show, enemies can become friends...

Another bright spot that winter was when Crossies was on the wireless, a "Works Wonders" programme. This was a programme on the BBC at lunch time from factory canteens, a different factory every day, and using local talent. I think the whole of Peterhead was listening to that programme. There were two local pipers on it, James Allan and James Watson, and a ladies choir drawn from different departments throughout the factory, Mr Fyvie singing "Bonnie Wee Thing" and Mrs Belle Summers, or Belle McCartney as we knew her, singing "An Auld Maid in a Garret". I wonder what the listeners in England thought about that one. I learned that song from Willum's wife, Jeannie but I couldn't understand why mother disapproved of it. Never mind, my renditions of the song were never in public and I probably had the more respectable version, the same one Belle sang in the "Works Wonders".

The threat of a German invasion was long past, so that winter, the Home Guard disbanded, or as they called it, "stood down". But you could still get fined for showing a light from your house. And there was a new crime that winter, one you could be up in front of the Sheriff for. And it was? Hard to believe now, but the crime was feeding oatmeal to animals. Oatmeal was for humans, as porridge, oatcakes, or stuffing, or anything our mothers could make of it, but not - definitely not - for pigs or chickens. Giving oatmeal to animals was forbidden!

As we went into the spring of 1945, some of our prisoners-of-war were being released, mainly from POW camps freed by the advancing Russians. Some of the men had been prisoners since St Valery, others from the North African fighting. And it had an almost surreal quality to it - though I'd never heard the term in those days - that along with those yellow envelopes announcing a loved one wounded or killed on duty, there were other yellow envelopes announcing that freed prisoners-of-war were coming home.

In May, arrangements were being made to celebrate Victory in Europe, or VE Day. Bells would ring, ships' hooters would sound, flags would fly, and we were impatient for Victory to be announced. It seemed to be dragging out because there was word that Hitler was dead and another man was the leader of Germany, and he was negotiating surrender terms, but it had to be unconditional surrender, and although some German armies had already surrendered, others were holding out.

But eventually, Mr Churchill went on the radio one afternoon - Tuesday, 8th May - and the King spoke that evening - and we all heard them on the wireless -the War was over and we had won. But not quite over, for there was still Japan, and they would never surrender. They would fight to the last man, woman and child.

There was a victory parade at the end of May and it poured with rain, then a victory gala in the Recreation Park and Barclay Park in June, and the sun shone for it. The town lights were switched on at the end of May and we saw the leerie again, a man who went round with a light on the end of a long pole lighting the gas street-lamps. But despite the celebrations, there was still Japan, and in our family, we knew that meant that Willum and Sandy would be going out to take part in its invasion. The thing is, that invasion would be a slaughter, both of defenders and invaders, them and us, because if the Japs fought so fanatically to protect a foreign island far from home, how would they fight to defend their sacred homeland. And their king they worshipped as their god.

One evening in August, mother was dragged off to the **Playhouse** by Jess and Jeannie, "to get their minds off things", as they said - she never went willingly to the picters - and father and I were alone in the house and listening to the nine o'clock news. Then we heard the startling news, and things would never be the same again. A new kind of bomb, about a thousand times stronger than the heaviest bomb dropped over Germany, had been dropped on the Japanese city of Hiroshima. I was thrilled, excited. It meant the Japs would have to surrender. There would be no invasion. And Willum and Sandy need not go to the Pacific. Great! I could hardly wait to tell mother about it. And so the excitement of that new development in the war against Japan gripped us all. But would the Japanese surrender because of one bomb? Supposing it was the only bomb we had - and we had used up our "secret weapon"? But then, days later, came the news of another super-bomb, this time on Nagasaki. And now we knew it was only a matter of time before the Japanese did the unthinkable, and actually surrendered, unconditionally. And so they did, and saved millions of lives in the process.

VJ - "Victory over Japan" Night - was a disappointment. We burnt nearly every wooden gate in Ives Park and Ugie Park on our bonfires, and an uncountable number of fish boxes from yards on Wilson Road - now known as Wilson Street - and a large amount of ship's timbers Abbie Milne had been collecting for his firewood business. But through it all, it poured with rain. Then we went down to Drummer's Corner and there was dancing, a band on the steps of the **Regal**, and an accordionist and a cornet player I think, on the roof of the air-raid shelter across from the cinema. These musicians took turn about providing music for the people who were dancing in the street, and ships horns were blowing, bells were ringing, along the seafront was a necklace of bonfires, and the rain was pouring. It was a gey drookit end to the War. Eventually my enthusiasm for Victory was diluted and I sloshed off home about midnight. In the joy of Victory, something of our hatred for the Enemy was forgotten.

Instead, there was sadness about all those people killed. Peterhead and Fraserburgh had each suffered twenty-three air-raids, with a number of folk killed, but Aberdeen, with its 34 air-raids was the most raided city in Scotland, though not the most heavily bombed. That would have been

Glasgow and Clydebank. I had learnt in my fight with my class-mate, how an enemy could become a friend. Perhaps there was the promise of a better future in that, maybe a chance for peace. Time would tell.

This Index of Civilian Casualties in the north-east of Scotland during World War II was compiled with the co-operation and permission of the Scottish National War Memorial Trust, and acknowledgement is paid the Trust for its help. The Index is laid out geographically and chronologically

City of Aberdeen   1940

Stewart, John (35) 405 Anderson Drive North, Injured 13/2/40 @ Loch St, died 15/2/40 @ RI

George, George (72) "Merlebank" Wellington Rd 27/4/40 @ "Merlebank" Wellington Rd

Mortimer, James (58) 89 Westburn Rd, 31/4/40 @ Kittybrewster Railway Station

Adam, Allan (42) 30 Urquhart Rd, 12/7/40 @ Hall & R Shipyard, York St
Anderson, James (55) 15 North Square, Footdee, Injured 12/7/40, @ Hall & R Shipyard, died same day @ RI
Baxter, William Leiper, (22) ARP, 27 Stafford St, 12/7/40 & Hall & R Shipyard, York St
Bissett, Gordon McKay (46) 33 Union Grove, 12/7/40 @ York St
Chalmers, Peter Cable (49)16 Ruthrieston Crescent 12/7/40 @ Hall R Shipyard, York St
Cromar, George Alexander (70) Matthews Quay, 12/7/40 @ York St
Currie, James (51) 4 Loirston Place, Injured 12/7/40 @ Hall R Shipyard, York St, died same day @ RI
Davidson, Alexander (66) 2 Bannermill St 12/7/40 @ York St
Geddes, Alexander Noble (40) 14 Pocra Quay, 12/7/40 @ Hall R Shipyard, York St
Gordon,. David (42) 8 Craigton Terrace 12/7/40 @ Hall R Shipyard @ York St
Gray, Charles Porter (47) Girdlestone Place, Torry 12/7/40 @ Hall R Shipyard, York St
Greig, Charles (58) 6 Powis Circle, 12/7/40 @ York St
Kinnaird, James Ross (30) 132 Don St, Woodside 12/7/40 @ Hall R Shipyard, York St
Leighton, William (64) 88 Urquhart Rd 12/7/40 @ York St
McKay, William (39) 53 Tullos Crescent 12/7/40 @ Hall R Shipyard, York St
McKenzie, Hugh David John George (59) 2 Girdlestone Place, Torry 12/7/40 @ York St
McPherson, James (19) 52 Mile End Ave, 12/7/40 @ York St
McTavish, William (27) 72 Mansefield Rd 12/7/40 @ York St
Pirie, Francis William Fisher (46) 7 Seaton Gardens, 12/7/40 @ York St
Pyper, John (41) 74 Park St 12/7/40 @ York St
Robertson, James (38) 126 Rosemount Place 12/7/40 @ Hall R Shipyard, York St
Robertson, James (formerly Begg, James Murray) (72) 19 York St, 12/7/40 @ York St
Sedgwick, Richard (76) 2 York St, Injured 12/7/40 @ York St died 15/8/40 @ RI
Sutherland, Thomas Dickson (31) 101 Commerce St, Injured 12/7/40 @ Hall R Shipyard, York St, died same day @ RI
Thomson, John (25) 125 West North St, 12/7/40 @ York St
Tosh, Thomas Park (31) 46 York Place, 12/7/40 @ York St
Webster, George Lovie (14) 9 1/2 York St, 12/7/40 @ York St
Webster, Ronald Milne (26) 86 Don St, Woodside, 12/7/40 @ York St
Webster, William Murray (29) 3 Firhill Place, 12/7/40 @ York St

Leys, Thomas Mulloy (27) 8 Kilgour Ave 12/7/40 @ RI
McCoss, James Rennof Bruce (49) Air Raid Warden, 4 Rosehill Terrace, Injured 12/7/40 @ 567 King St, died same day @ RI
Mortimer, James Duncan (57) Seaman, Merchant Navy, 88 Grampian Circle, Injured 12/7/40 @ Footdee, died 13/7/40 @ RI
Robertson, Norman McLeod (37) 57 Logie Place, 12/7/40 @ RI

Shirriffs, Elizabeth (69) 42 Forbesfield Rd 28/8/40 @ Forbesfield Rd

Buchan, Francis Munro (19) 55 Wellington Rd, 4/11/40 @ 55 Wellington Rd
Buchan, Robert Schultze (26) 55 Wellington Rd, 4/11/40 @ 55 Wellington Rd
Fraser, William (17) 55 Wellington Rd, 4/11/40 @ 55 Wellington Rd
Knowles, William (6) 55 Wellington Rd, Injured 4/11/40 @ 55 Wellington Rd, died 5/11/40 @ RI

Gillham, Harry (51) 37 Donbank Terrace, Injured 15/12/40 @ Dyce Aerodrome, died 16/12/40 @ RI

Aberdeen City   1941

Birnie, Charles (56) 49 Powis Place, 13/2/41 @ Loch St
Booth, Agnes Ross (19) 20A Young St, Injured 13/2/41 @ Loch St, died 18/2/41 @ RI
Brannen, Alexander (68) 85 Loch St 13/2/41 @ Loch St
Brannen, Edith (5) 85 Loch St, 13/2/41 @ Loch St
Brannen, Isabella (65) 85 Loch St, 13/2/41 @ Loch St
Fraser, William (26) Strabathie Cottages, Bridge of Don 13/2/41 @ Loch St
Gravells, Fred (48) 33 Causeway End, 13/2/41 @ Loch St
Grigor, James (58) 21 North Silver St 13/2/41 @ Lochside Bar, Loch St
Innes, Annabella (36) 85 Loch St, 13/2/41 @ 85 Loch St
Innes, George Alexander (64) 85 Loch St, 13/2/41 @ 85 Loch St
Innes, George Alexander (2) 85 Loch St, 13/2/41 @ 85 Loch St
Kelman, Robert Whyte (39) 5 Bath St, 13/2/41 @ Loch St
Pirie, Charles, (56) 12 John St, Injured 13/2/41 @ Loch St, died same day @ RI
Ronald, Robert Paterson (45) 121 Union Grove, 13/2/41 @ Loch St
Symon, Alexander Gordon (37) 18 Logie Avenue, Woodside,13/2/41 @ Loch St
Symon, Gordon McQueen (52) 12 Powis Circle 13/2/41 @ Loch St
Christie, Colin Hunter (6) 79 Hutcheon St, 13/2/41 @ Hutcheon St
Fraser, William (32) 7 Pittodrie Place, 13/2/41 @ John St

Davidson, George Gordon (48) Fire Watcher, 14 Kintore Place, Injured 15/2/41 @ Northern Hotel, died same day @ RI

Watson, Alistair (3) 38 Urquhart Rd, 20/4/41 @ Gallowhill Gardens, Golf Rd

Beaton, Charles Edward (57) 67 Mansefieldd Place 6/6/41 @ Greyhope Rd

Gibb, William (71) Fire Guard - 102 Walker Rd, Torry - 21/7/41 @ North Eastern Ice Co, Commercial Rd
Philip, George (64) 5 Dee Place, 21/7/41 @ North Eastern Ice Co, Commercial Rd

Deans, Alexander (11) 17 Don Place, Woodside, 24/7/41 @ 17 Don Place
Wilson, Annie (55) 371 Great Northern Rd, Woodside, 24/7/41 @ 371 Great Northern Rd
Ross, William (?) 8 Menzies Rd, Injured 2/8/41 @ 8 Menzies Rd, died 17/3/44 @ Old Mill (Annexe) Hospital
Macdonald, Thomas Yule (17) 8 Menzies Rd, Injured 8/8/41 @ 3 Menzies Rd, died same day @ RI

Chapman, William (33) Bannermill Lodge, Bannermill Road 19/8/41 @ Bannermill Lodge

Aberdeen City   1942

Milton, James (17) Church Buildings, Gallowgate, Injured 25/4/42 @ Church Buildings, died 26/4/42 @ RI

Robertson, Sylvia Mary Lily (2) 26/4/42 @ 22 Summerfield Terrace

Dow, James Forbes Cusiter (49) ARP Rescue Service, 98 School Rd - Injured 7/8/42 @ Torry, died 8/8/42 @ RI
Eddie, Charles William (16) Home Guard 164 Victoria Rd, Injured 7/8/42 @ 208 Market St, died 8/8/42 @ FAP Walker Rd
Smith, Edward Harry (17) 13 Walker Rd, Torry 7/8/42 @ FAP Walker Rd
Mennie, Alvin Burnett (22) ARP Rescue Service, 21 Stonehaven Rd, Bridge of Dee, Injured 7/8/42 @ Poynernook Rd; died 16/8/42 @RI
Park, Mary Morrison (32) FAP Nurse BRCS Section Leader, 63 High St, 7/8/42 @ Poynernook Rd
Thom, George Smith (44) Fire Guard 17 South Square, Injured 7/8/42 @ Poynernook Rd, died same day in ambulance between Palmerston Road and RI
Watt, James (33) ARP Rescue Service, 14 Roslin St, Injured 7/8/42 @ South Market St, died 8/8/42 @ RI

Aberdeen City   1943

Barclay, Edith Annie (43) 48 Bedford Rd,21/4/43 @ 48 Bedford Rd
Cox, Wiliamina Duncan (22) 60 Bedford Rd, 21/4/43 @ 60 Bedford Rd
Cox, Freda Gillan (3) 60 Bedford Rd,21/4/43 @ 60 Bedford Rd
Cox, Frederick Gillan (17 Months) 60 Bedford Rd, Injured 21/4/43 @ 60 Bedford Rd, died 22/4/43 @ RI
Cox, John Forbes Gillan (5 months) 60 Bedford Rd,21/4/43 @ 60 Bedford Rd
Duncan, Ann Grant (43) 77 Bedford Rd 21/4/43 @ 77 Bedford Rd
Duncan, John Sandison (58) 55 Bedford Rd 21/4/43 @ 60 Bedford Rd
Mackay, Helen Catherine (35) 60 Bedford Rd 21/4/43 @ 60 Bedford Rd
Mackay, Sheila (3) 60 Bedford Rd, 21/4/43 @ 60 Bedford Rd
Mackay, William (38) Fire Guard, 60 Bedford Rd 21/4/43 @60 Bedford Rd
Moir, Catherine Craigie (43) Fire Guard, 60 Bedford Rd, 21/4/43 @ 60 Bedford Rd
Moir, John Mutch (9) 60 Bedford Rd 21/4/43 @ 60 Bedford Rd
Paterson, Eileen Watson (18) 77 Bedford St 21/4/43 @ 77 Bedford St
Porter, Alexander Anderson (40) 60 Bedford Rd 21/4/43 @ 60 Bedford Rd
Porter, Jessie Anne Wilhelmina Wilson (41) 60 Bedford Rd 21/4/43 @ 60 Bedford Rd
Porter, June Lewis (9) 60 Bedford Rd, 21/4/43 @ 60 Bedford Rd
Porter, Robert Alexander (17) 60 Bedford Rd, 21/4/43 @ 60 Bedford Rd
Reid, Gordon (15) 48 Bedford Rd, 21/4/43 @ 48 Bedford Road
Reid, Robert (10) 48 Bedford Rd 21/4/43 @ 48 Bedford Rd
Walker, George (18) FAP Member 75 Bedford Rd 21/4/43 @ 75 Bedford Rd
Walker, Isabella Craig (46) FAP Member 75 Bedford Rd 21/4/43 @ 75 Bedford Rd
Walker, James (53) 75 Bedford Rd 21/4/43 @ 75 Bedford Rd
Watt, Christian (70) 60 Bedford Rd 21/4/43 @ 60 Bedford Rd
Watt, Elizabeth (74) 60 Bedford Rd, 21/4/43 @ 60 Bedford Rd
Forbes, Catherine (34) 33 Brown St, Woodside 21/4/43 @ 33 Brown St
Forbes, William (35) 33 Brown St, Woodside 21/4/43 @ 33 Brown St
Forbes, Kathleen (10 months) 33 Brown St, Woodside 21/4/43 @ 33 Brown St
Fraser, Jessie (60) 33 Brown St 21/4/43 @ 33 Brown St
Philip, James (45) 37 Brown St, Injured 21/4/43 @ 37 Brown St, died 23/4/43 @ RI
Black, Elizabeth Mary (43) 72A Catherine St 21/4/43 @ 72A Catherine St
Duthie, Helen (69) 72A Catherine St 21/4/43 @ 72A Catherine St
Knowles, Margaret Ann (67) 72A Catherine St 21/4/43 @ 72A Catherine St
Cameron, Norman (51) Cpl Home Guard 80 Cattofield Place 21/4/43 @ Cattofield Place
Hunter, Agnes Mary (28) 53 Cattofield Place 21/4/43 @ Cattofield Place
Sutton, Elizabeth Anne (54) WVS 7 Urquhart Rd 21/4/43 @ 53 Cattofield Place
Stephen, James Hutcheon (76) 9 Cattofield Gardens, Injured 21/4/43 @ 9 Cattofield Gdns died 25/4/43 @ RI
Clark, Elizabeth Johnston (27) 33 Charles St, 21/4/43 @ 33 Charles St
Clark, William John Anderson (3) 33 Charles St 21/4/43 @ 33 Charles St
Conner, James (40) Home Guard 10 Ferrier Crescent 21/4/43 @ 33 Charles St
Duncan, Agnes (74) 31 Charles St 21/4/43 @ 31 Charles St
Duncan, Andrew (82)31 Charles St, 21/4/43 @ 31 Charles St
Kelbie, Mary Ann Mullen (59) 33 Charles St 21/4/43 @ 33 Charles St
Massie, Elizabeth (37) Fire Guard 33 Charles St 21/4/43 @ 33 Charles St
Newman, Barbara (36) Fire Guard 33 Charles St 21/4/43 @ 33 Charles St
Newman, Barbara McBeth (59) 33 Charles St 21/4/43 @ 33 Charles St
Newman, Ernest Shand (4) 33 Charles St 21/4/43 @ 33 Charles St
Newman, Isabella (23) Fire Guard 33 Charles St 21/4/43 @ 33 Charles St
Newman, Mary Wemyss (26) Fire Guard 33 Charles St 21/4/43 @ 33 Charles St
Wallis, Charles (72) 45 Charles St, Injured 21/4/43 @ 45 Charles St, died 23/4/43 @ RI
Forsyth, Mary Jack (29) 20 Church St, Woodside 21/4/43 @ 20 Church St
Forsyth, Francis Smith (16months) 20 Church St, Woodside 21/4/43 @ 20 Church St
Reid, Isabella Bruce (64) 299 Clifton Rd 21/4/43 @ Clifton Rd
Brand, William (26) Fire Guard 121 Rosemount Place, 21/4/43 @ 26 Cornhill Rd
Law, Elizabeth Jane (37) 15 Chapel St, Peterhead 21/4/43 @ 26 Cornhill Rd
Russell, Beatrice (40) RMPA Fire Guard, 29 Ashvale Place, 21/4/43 @ Royal Mental Hospital
Simpson, Lizzie (31) Fire Guard, 2 Calton Terrace 21/4/43 @ 26 Cornhill Rd
Donaldson, John (57) 19 Cummings Park Rd, Woodside, 21/4/43 @ 19 Cummings Park Rd
Calder, Evelyn Milne (34) 6 Elmbank Rd, 21/4/43 @ Elmbank Rd
Calder, William (34) Leading Fireman, NFS 6 Elmbank Rd 21/4/43 @ 6 Elmbank Rd
Calder, Evelyn Anne (3) 6 Elmbank Rd, 21/4/43 @ Elmbank Rd

Craib, John Donald (21) 6 Elmbank Rd 21//4/43 @ 6 Elmbank Rd
Ferguson, Agnes (47) 6 Elmbank Rd, 21/4/43 @ 6 Elmbank Rd
Ferguson, William (56) 6 Elmbank Rd 21/4/43 @ 6 Elmbank Rd
Ferguson, Margaret Hepburn (16) 6 Elmbank Rd, 21/4/43 @ 6 Elmbank Rd
Ferrier, James (67) 6 Elmbank Rd, 21/4/43@ 6 Elmbank Rd
Ferrier, Lizzie Leys Collie (68) 6 Elmbank Rd, 21/4/43 @ 6 Elmbank Rd
McRobb, Jennie Harvey (26) 6 Elmbank Rd 21/4/43 @ 6 Elmbank Rd
Mitchell, Annie (38) 6 Elmbank Rd 21/4/43 @ 6 Elmbank Rd
Mitchell, Kathleen Ann Stalker (5) 6 Elmbank Rd 21/4/43 @ 6 Elmbank Rd
Stove, Joan (50) 6 Elmbank Rd, 12/4/43 @ 6 Elmbank Rd
Watson, Ethel (36) 6 Elmbank Rd 21/4/43@ 6 Elmbank Rd
Watson, William Allen (43) 6 Elmbank Rd 21//4/43 @ 6 Elmbank Rd
Wallace, Ernest Murray (10) 41 Erskine St, Injured 21/4/43 @ Erskine St, died 24/4/43 @ RI
Wallace, James Valentine (17) 6 King's Cross Terrace 21/4/43 @ King's Cross Terrace
McGillivary, Hector (32) Member of LNER Fire Brigade, 7 Hill St, 21/4/43 @ Kittybrewster Railway Stn
Taylor, Alfred (23) 3 Bannomill St 21/4/43 @ Kittybrewster Rly Stn
Simpson, William (55) 5 Froghall Terrace, 21/4/43 @ Kittybrewster Rly Stn
Yeats, Stuart McLean (40) 9 Newton Terrace, Bucksburn, 21/4/43 @ Kittybrewster Rly Stn
Gibb, William (39) 22 Powis Place, 21/4/43 @ Powis Place
Grant, Charles Henderson (62) 32 Powis Place 21/4/43 @ 10 1/2 Powis Place
Guyan, John Webster (47) 30 Powis Place, Injured 21/4/43 @ Aberdeen, died 5/6/43 @ Strathcathro Hospital
Murray, Jessie Watt (60) 30 Powis Place, 21/4/43 @30 Powis Place
Sinclair, Jane (38) 6 Powis Place, Injured 21/4/43 @ Powis Circle died 22/4/43 @ RI
Cameron, Margaret (76) 34 Tanfield Walk, 21/4/43 @ Printfield Walk
Moir, Westland (44) 106 Provost Rust Drive 21/4/43, @ 106 Provost Rust Drive
Webster, Andrew (70) 9 Stafford St, 21/4/43 @ 9 Stafford St
Symon, Emily Amelia Caroline (18) 18 Logie Avenue, Woodside 21/4/43 @ Summer St
Brown, James Willocks (43) Lieut, Home Guard 119 Western Road, Hilton, 21/4/43 @ 119 Western Rd
Brown, Angus Webster (3) 119 Western Rd, 21/4/43 @ 119 Western Rd
Brown, Mabel Jane Edith (46) 119 Western Rd 21/4/43 @ 119 Western Rd
Burr, James Hector (17) ARP Messenger, 100 Western Rd, Hilton, 21/4/43 @ Hilton Drive
Flett, Archibald Duncan (61) 115 Western Rd, 21/4/43 @ Western Rd
Leggat, Robert (49) 117 Western Rd, 21/4/43 @ 117 Western Rd
Merchant, Jane Ann (30) 115 Western Rd, Hilton 21/4/43 @ 115 Western Rd
Webster, Catherine Helen (54) 20 Jamaica St, 21/4/43 @ 119 Western Rd, Woodside

Davidson, Joseph Henderson (39) ARP Section Leader, 106 Morningside Avenue, 22/7/43 @ Queens Rd

Yeoman, William Cowan (69) Fire Guard, 7 Great Northern Rd, 11/11/43 @ Woodside Works

Fraserburgh   1940

Herd, Mary Jane (18) "Mhor House" Finlayson St, 13/8/40 @ "Mhor House" Finlayson St
Ralph, Mary (75) 7 Queen Mary St, Injured 13/8/40 @ 7 Queen Mary St, died 14/8/40 @ RI
Ralph, Thomas (80) 7 Queen Mary St, Injured 13/8/40 @ 7 Queen Mary St, died 23/9/40 @ Kincardine House Auxiliary Hospital

Birnie, James (42) 4 Caroline Place Injured 5/11/40 Fraserburgh, died 8/11/40 @ RI
Barclay, William (40) 31 Manse St, 5/11/40 @ 2 Kirkbrae
Crawford, Charles James (19) 46 Broadsea 5/11/40 @ 2 Kirkbrae
Duthie, Alexander Thain (32) 17 Castle St 5/11/40 @ 2 Kirkbrae
Duthie, Gilbert (31) 49 Dennyduff Rd, 5/11/40 @ 2 Kirkbrae
Kemp, David Hay (23) 12 Union St Lane, Bridgend, Perth @ 2 Kirkbrae
McLeman, Alexander Peter (24) 50 Main St, Broadsea, 5/11/40 @ 2 Kirkbrae
Malley, Edward (25) 36 Broadsea, 5/11/40 @ 2 Kirkbrae
O'Hara, Lily (44) 4 Kirkbrae, 5/11/40 @ 2 Kirkbrae
O'Hara, Peter (47) 4 Kirkbrae, 5/11/40 @ 2 Kirkbrae
Reid, Alexander (19) 14 Queen Mary St, 5/11/40 @ 2 Kirkbrae
Rogan, John (28) 35 Carnegie St, Edinburgh, 5/11/40 @ 2 Kirkbrae
Stewart, John Pennycook (35) 45 Canal St, Perth, 5/11/40 @ 2 Kirkbrae
Walker, Charles Downie (43) 52 Broadsea, 5/11/40 @ 2 Kirkbrae
Wilson, Thomas Clark (28) 86 Gourlay St, Springburn St, Glasgow, 5/11/40 @ Kirkbrae
Buchan, Alexander (59) 53 High St 5/11/40 @ 7 Broad St
Cruickshank, Jessie Duthie (24) 11 Brucklay St, Rosehearty, 5/11/40 @ 3 Broad St
Cruickshank, James (29) 11 Brucklay St, Rosehearty, 5/11/40 @ 3 Broad St
Glennie, Edith (24) 3 Broad St, 5/11/40 @ 3 Broad St
Glennie, Leslie John (28) 3 Broad St, 5/11/40 @ 3 Broad St
Glennie, Edith (5) 3 Broad St, 5/11/40 @ 3 Broad St
Noble, Andrew (31) 9 Caroline Place, 5/11/40 @ Broad St

Fraserburgh   1941

Dunbar, Jessie Ann (37) 6 Commerce St, Injured 5/4/41 @ Maconnachies Factory, died 6/4/41 @ RI
Michael, Christian Smith (59) 92A Shore St, Injured 5/4/41 @ Maconnachies Factory, died 6/4/41 @ RI
Sim, Elizabeth (32) 30 Noble St, 5/4/41 @ Preserving Works, Bath St
Simpson, Jean Booth (34) 15 Cross St, 5/4/41 @ Preserving Works, Bath St
Nicol, Agnes (53) 124 Harbour Head, Gardenstown, Banffshire, Injured 5/4/41 @ Fraserburgh, died 8/4/41 @ RI

Bowie, Jessie Sutherland (36) 67 High St, 17/4/41 @ 28 Castle St
Dunbar, Millicent (5) 28 Castle St, Injured 17/4/41 died 18/4/41 @ Sick Children's Hospital, Aberdeen
McLeod, Katie Darling (24) 7 Greig St, Inverness, 17/4/41 @ 28 Castle St
Melvin, Jessie (38) 30 Castle St, 17/4/41 @ 30 Castle St
Mitchell, Catherine Sutherland (64) 28 Castle St, 17/4/41 @ 28 Castle St
Reid, Isabella Ann (42) Sandhole Cottages, Memsie, 17/4/41 @ 30 Castle St
Sinclair, Rachel Macdonald (31) 30 Castle St, 17/4/41 @ 30 Castle St

Smith, James (74) 17 Commerce St, 26/6/41 @ 17 Commerce St
Smith, Helen Brown (58) 17 Commerce St, 26/6/41 @ 17 Commerce St

Fraserburgh   1943

Kerr, Laurence McKay (11) 57 School St, 20/2/43 @ 59 School St

Peterhead   1940
Smith, George (65) 68 York St, 22/8/40 @ 68 York St
Smith, Leslie Wilson (5) 68 York St, 22/8/40 @ 68 York St
Wyness, William (56) Air Raid Warden, 61 Landale Rd, 22/8/40 @ 68 York St

Peterhead   1941
Hamilton, Thomas (74) 43 North St, 10/8/41 @ 43 North St
Murray, Jane Will (23) 43 North St, 10/8/41 @ 43 North St
Murray, Myrna (7 months) 43 North St, 10/8/41 @ 43 North St
Keith, Annie (71) 47 Queen St, 10/8/41 @ 47 Queen St
Taylor, Robina (59) BRCS Bronze Medals with Bars for First Aid and Home Nursing, FAP Auxiliary
Nurse, 27 Constitution St, 10/8/41 @ FAP St Peter St

Barron, Isabella Whyte (69) 11 James St, 29/9/41 @ 11 James St
Barron, William (69) 11 James St, 29/9/41 @ 11 James St
Cameron, Edith Cormack (6) 5 James St, 29/9/41 @ 5 James St
Cameron, James Lees (2) 5 James St, 29/9/41 @ 5 James St
Cameron, Jessie Scott (40) 5 James St, 29/9/41 @ 5 James St
Cameron, Lorna (12 months) 5 James St, 29/9/41 @ 5 James St
Chalmers, Henry Charles (7) 11 James St, 29/9/41 @ 11 James St
Chalmers, Marjory Angus (4) 11 James St, 29/9/41 @ 11 James St
Chalmers, Sheila (11) 11 James St, 29/9/41 @ 11 James St
Cormack, Jessie (64) 11 James St, 29/9/41 @ 11 James St
Duncan, Agnes Clark (20) 56 Queen St, 29/9/41 @ 9 James St
Duncan, Isabella Nora Hutchison (38) 8 James St, 29/9/41 @ 11 James St
Duncan, John McQueen (19) 56 Queen St, 29/9/41 @ 9 James St
Duncan, Margaret Isabella (17) 8 James St, 29/9/41 @ 11 James St
Lacey, Andrewina Bruce Geddes (5) 9 James St, 29/9/41 @ 9 James St
Lacey, Margaret Buchan (11) 9 James St, 29/9/41 @ 9 James St
Lacey, May Buchan (3) 9 James St, 29/9/41 @ 9 James St
Lacey, Sarah Bruce (33) 9 James St, 29/9/41 @ 9 James St
Lawson, Jane Anne Brown Porter (6) 9 James St, 29/9/41 @ 9 James St
McKay, Douglas (3) 9 James St, 29/9/41 @ 9 James St
McKay, Gladys Wilson (7) 9 James St, 29/9/41 @ 9 James St
McKay, Jean (36) 9 James St, 29/9/41 @ 9 James St
Mackie, Alexander (47) 9 James St, 29/9/41 @ 9 James St
Mackie, Isabella Jane (48) 9 James St, 29/9/41 @ 9 James St
Milne, Williamina Elizabeth (50) 60 Longate, 29/9/41 @ 11 James St
Shepherd, Henry Charles (63) 7 James St, 29/9/41 @ 11 James St
Shepherd, Marjaret Jane Craig (60) 7 James St, 29/9/41 @ 11 James St
Strachan, Williamina (45) 9 James St, 29/9/41 @ 9 James St
Watson, Helenora (46) 9 James St, 29/9/41 @ 9 James St
Watson, William (50) Injured 29/9/41 @ 9 James St, died 30/9/41 @ RI

Rosehearty   1942

Bruce, Alicia West (70) 27 Pitsligo St, 29/1/42 @ 27 Pitsligo St
Chalmers, Mary Tait (29) 25 North St, Fraserburgh , 29/1/42 @ 25 Pitsligo St
Chalmers, Norma Mary (4) 25 North St, Fraserbugh, 29/1/42 @ 25 Pitsligo St
Duncan, Dorothy Dunbar (14) 12 Queen St, 29/1/42 @ 25 Pitsligo St
Gunn, James McKenzie (10) 25 Pitsligo St, 29/1/42 @ 25 Pitsligo St
Gunn, Marjorie (32) 25 Pitsligo St, 29/9/42 @ 25 Pitsligo St
Leitch, Mary (11) 41 Appleby St, Hamilton Hill, Glasgow, 29/1/42 @ 25 Pitsligo St
Noble, Betsy Mary (39) 25 Pitsligo St, 29/1/42 @ 25 Pitsligo St
Noble, Florence (8) 25 Pitsligo St, 29/1/42 @ 25 Pitsligo St
Noble, George (3) 25 Pitsligo St. 29/1/42 @ 25 Pitsligo St
Noble, William (10) 25 Pitsligo St, 29/1/42 @ 25 Pitsligo St
Innes, Catherine Fowlie (60) 25 Brucklay St, 29/1/42 @ 25 Brucklay St

County of Aberdeen   1941

Gray, James ((78) Bay View House, Cruden Bay, 2/4/41 @ Brickworks, Cruden Bay
McLeod, John (58) Royal Observer Corps, Dunby Cottage, Cruden Bay, 2/4/41 @ Brickworks, Cruden Bay

Pirie, James William (57) Royal Observer Corps, 3 Manse Terrace, Boddam, Peterhead. Injured 16/5/41 @ Observer Post, Stirling Hill, Boddam, died 17/5/41 @ 3 Manse Terrace

Brodie, Robert (59) 3 Windsor Place, Aberdeen, 24/7/41 @ RAF Aerodrome, Dyce

County of Aberdeen   1943

Grant, Helen Donaldson (18) 43 Main St, Rhynie, 21/4/43 (see Aberdeen List - 21/4/43)

County of Aberdeen   1944

Ingram, Alexander John (36) Dalgarno Croft, Balthangie, 12/7/44 @ Dalgarno Croft

Macduff   1945

Chalmers, John Shepherd (49) Royal Observer Corps, 35 Clergy St. 28/1/45 @ Macduff

County of Kincardine

Young, Charles William (43) 48 Shipley Avenue, Newcastle-upon-Tyne, 7/7/41 @ Kempstonehill, Cowie

Lindsay, John (63) Nether Wyndings, Fetteresso - 11/11/44 @ Nether Wyndings